Live Life, Love Food

A cook's book

Live Life, Love Food

NONI CAMPBELL-HORNER

●● **PAGE TWO** BOOKS

Cataloguing in publication information is
available from Library and Archives Canada.
ISBN 978-1-989603-84-0 (hardcover)
ISBN 978-1-77458-033-2 (paperback)

Page Two
www.pagetwo.com

Edited by Amanda Lewis
Copyedited by Melissa Edwards
Proofread by Alison Strobel
Cover and interior design by Fiona Lee
Cover and interior illustrations by Noni Campbell-Horner

Printed and bound in Canada by Friesens

20 21 22 23 24   5 4 3 2 1

For Don,
who has always journeyed with me

Noni's Garden

We leave cool of forest
View of ocean
Up through fern, watch for nettle
Rival birds for chatter
Underfoot soft with moss, earth, leaf
Bridge of cedar
Leads to perfumed Tuscan gardens
Sniff roses, iris, honeysuckle
Inspect vegetables, trees, ripening figs
Beg for strawberries, plan supper salad
Shun caterpillars
Swing in hot sun
Become quiet listening to buzz of bees
Heat sends us back to
Breezy ocean shore

Marjorie Phillips
Pender Island, June 2011

Contents

Stories in This Book

Creativity requires the courage to let go of certainties.

ERICH FROMM

About This Book

I AM AN INTUITIVE PERSON. Intuition and improvisation have led me to joy, and they have also carried me through some very dark times.

For me, life and food dance together.

Breaking bread with another allows the sharing of life stories and experiences in both happy and sad times. Food is a catalyst for social interaction, and has been since the beginning of time.

Many cooks use recipes with precision. I do not cook that way. I love recipe books and read them often (a favourite is *The Flavor Bible* by Karen Page and Andrew Dornenburg), but then I go on with my own creations. I love mucking about in the kitchen, and sometimes the results aren't what I had in mind. There is always learning with creativity.

In this book you will find ingredients and recipes—some with precise amounts and instructions, some with just some loose suggestions and a few tips on how I often make them. For each of these recipes, I offer you an invitation to follow the instructions using your own intuition. They are meant as a guide, a gift of ideas.

You may wonder why I have included short stories throughout the book. Just like I do when I cook, in my everyday life I have let my curiosity take me to new and interesting places. These stories are about moments in my life that were born from my curiosity and intuition, and many are connected to food and friends in some way. I am sharing some of these moments with you.

Enjoy!

NONI

Breakfasts and Baking

Morning Fruit
THREE WAYS

I really like fruit toppings for porridge, crêpes, pancakes and waffles. They are easy to make and freeze well. You can use blueberries or raspberries with a little lemon juice, or apples with a bit of cinnamon and nutmeg, or your favourite mix of strawberries, plums, cherries, mangos, oranges or bananas—just wash and prepare before following the recipes. If you can use organic fruit, all the better. I use frozen or canned to augment whatever fresh fruit I can get. And I always use figs, either fresh or dried—they are a must!

FIRST WAY

Pour about 2 tbsp of Triple Sec over the fruit and leave to sit for a bit at room temperature.

SECOND WAY

This second method comes from Kathy, an excellent brunch hostess. Cover the fruit with the juice and the rind of a lime, along with about 2 tbsp of maple syrup and some chopped fresh mint (about 5 or 6 leaves).

THIRD WAY

In a small pot, combine just a handful of your fruit (use your judgement—some fruits are better cooked longer, some less) with 1 to 2 tbsp of cornstarch and a small scoop of sugar. Cook until glossy, then remove from the heat and add the remaining fruit, along with some vanilla or star anise.

Blin

Blin is a name I created for this healthy, creamy condiment. I serve it with fruit, and with waffles, pancakes or crêpes. I love this stuff!

★ **A yogurt cheese maker can be purchased at any cook shop.**

500 ml container cottage cheese

½ cup Greek yogurt or yogurt cheese (see page 265)

½ container mascarpone

¼ cup sugar (go light, you don't need much)

Rind from half a lemon

A few squirts of fresh lemon juice

Process the cottage cheese until it is really smooth. Add the yogurt cheese or Greek yogurt, mascarpone, sugar, lemon rind and lemon juice. Blend until creamy, then store in the refrigerator or freezer for later use.

Morning Walks

FRIENDS OFTEN ASK why we would ever get another dog after the kids were gone. "You are free at last to travel, enjoy your freedom—why oh why would you get another dog? A puppy, no less!" Misha, our new dog, is a jet-black Belgian shepherd. He resembles an American wolf and howls like a black bear. Our daughter has lovingly dubbed him "Mishtar, king of the dogs." He is certainly king of something—probably our hearts.

Because Misha is in our lives we do morning walks. What started as a task has become a joy. Without fail, every morning, no matter the weather, city or state of mind, we fall out of bed at about 6 a.m. to walk Misha. The trick to accomplishing early rising is not thinking. Do not think! Just move. Once we are out the door, a world of magic awaits us.

It is March 30, 2005, in Vancouver. I stumble out of bed at 6:04 a.m. No rain today, thank God! The sky is clear blue, the sun is rising. A beautiful day is ahead of us. There is time only for the basics—after all, the dog has been in all night and he is still a puppy, albeit a large one. No time to brush hair or teeth. On with the black cap, jacket, jeans and shades. Off we go!

The clear crisp morning greets us as we cross into the park. We are not the first ones out. A very large food wagon is set up beside the park. Breakfast is being served. Trucks and people are bustling around. I see a cop and ask what is going on. He explains that they are filming a candy commercial. There are about a dozen vehicles, including the food wagon and an ice cream/yogurt truck, plus four to six tents and at least sixty people milling around, taking up space on two streets and in the courtyard in between. Many of the people are wearing caps and shades, just like me. I wonder, do they have bedhead and sleep in their eyes too? As we pass through our park, leaving the making of a commercial behind, I am dismayed at the magnitude of equipment, people and effort that goes into creating one little candy commercial.

On any other day, the park has its morning regulars. Even without a watch, I'd know the time. The homeless man is rising and stretching beside a grocery cart piled high with his worldly treasures, just as he did at the same time and spot yesterday. An old woman glances over and Misha barks at her small white dog—he'd like to play! At the lights crossing West Fourth Avenue, I leave our park and enter the Granville Market area. We meet the same attractive, dark-skinned lady with the neat red and orange shoes—the same ones as yesterday. Nice shoes—I could ask her where she got them, but I don't.

Turning east along False Creek, we approach a pond. Truly a beautiful place of peace and tranquility, a place for Misha to stop and sniff. Me, I just drink in the sounds, smells and sights. The pond is home to Canada geese, turtles and mallard ducks. Large rocks surround the pond, with lush vegetation bursting forth. The tall trees around us are home to a variety of smaller birds, such as robins, sparrows and red-winged blackbirds. A hush surrounds us as we listen to the birds' morning songs.

Winding along our walk, I suddenly become aware of a fragrance, so strong and beautiful … if it could only be bottled! Searching, I find a small tree—a bush, really, with yellow flowers just opening. Witch hazel is my mystery fragrance. Next we come upon orange-faced daffodils, just opening. So fresh, strong and stately.

Turning for home, we cross a small bridge and head around a wooded area, where the smell of forest hits us smack in the middle of this large urban centre. A man holding a blue rubber band between both hands passes us—same time and place as yesterday. Must be some sort of hand or wrist exercise.

Back through the park, activity has picked up. People are using the park as a shortcut, carrying their lattes and umbrellas, rushing to catch buses or head to work. It is time for us to go home for our breakfast.

What a wonderful way to begin a day. I wonder if I would be doing this walk without our puppy.

Rhubarb and Blueberry Topping

This stuff is really good! I use it on pancakes and waffles, along with coconut/lime yogurt, but it could also top a sponge cake, panna cotta or custard.

2 large handfuls of chopped, washed rhubarb

⅓ cup sugar

2 tsp cornstarch

Sugar, to taste

Grated nutmeg

Glug of Madeira or maple syrup

Juice of ½ orange

1½ cups fresh blueberries

Roast the rhubarb with ⅓ cup sugar, then set aside, saving the juice. Combine the juice with cornstarch, a bit of sugar, the nutmeg and a good splash of Madeira or maple syrup. Cook until it is slightly thick and transparent. If it is too thick, just add a little orange juice as it cools. Finally, add the cooked rhubarb and blueberries.

Porridge

TWO WAYS

I love porridge! After walking Misha, all I want is a bowl of porridge and a latte. For either of my porridge recipes, I mix it in a large batch (except when I use quinoa, which must be rinsed before adding) and keep it in the fridge—this cuts down on prep time. I use walnuts, almonds, pecans, pumpkin seeds and sesame seeds with my porridge, along with whatever dried fruit I feel like.

★ Cook porridge in large batches, then cool and store in vacuum packs in individual serving sizes for future use. I always make my porridge in a good-quality rice cooker I bought at T&T Supermarket—no mess!

FIRST WAY

Traditional rolled oats
(not the quick-cooking variety)

Oatmeal

Wheat germ

Cornmeal

Oat bran

Quinoa (rinsed)

Toasted nuts and seeds, to taste

Dried fruit (such as figs, dates,
blueberries, cranberries or apricots)

Create a mix of the oats, oatmeal, wheat germ, cornmeal, oat bran and quinoa—the amounts of each can vary according to your preference, but they should total about 3 cups.

Scoop out about half a cup of the mixture, top with about 3 inches of water, and cook on your stovetop for about 5 minutes, or longer if you wish. As my cereal is cooking, I usually add some nuts and seeds and fresh blueberries or any other fruit or fruit sauce I have on hand—use whatever amount and mix you like.

SECOND WAY

Old-fashioned oatmeal

Organic quinoa (rinsed)

Red River Hot Cereal

Ground flax (a small amount)

Dried fruit or nuts of your choice

Handful of granola

Again, mix the grains to total about 5 cups. Cover the mixture with about 3 inches of water and cook—remember that quinoa takes a little longer, and you may need to add more water as you go. Serve topped with fruit and nuts. You can top the cooked cereal with granola as well, or even add the granola in as you cook the grains.

Banana Bread

A few years ago, I took our daughter Suzanne for a week of quality mother-daughter time at the Canyon Ranch spa in Arizona. They served us their famous banana bread. This recipe is as close as I've come to my memory of that delicious bread.

★ There are all kinds of flours—often, I'll swap in almond or oat flour to replace all-purpose flour. Experiment with a variety, but remember that with non-gluten flours you need to add a little more baking powder.

1½ to 1⅔ cups all-purpose flour

¾ to 1 cup sugar

A few twists of freshly grated nutmeg

1½ tsp baking powder

½ tsp baking soda

Cinnamon, to taste

Pinch of salt

About 3 to 4 ripe bananas, mashed

½ cup oil

2 eggs

3 tbsp unsweetened applesauce

Mix all of the dry ingredients together. In a separate bowl, mix the wet ingredients. Combine with as little mixing as possible until the dry ingredients are moist.

Bake in a greased loaf pan at 350 degrees for 35 minutes, then check. It may need a bit more time at a lower temperature (about 300 degrees).

Honey Oatmeal Bread

I created this bread in a quest for health. If you wish, you can top it with seeds and grains. I like toasted sesame, pumpkin and sunflower seeds.

1 tbsp instant yeast

½ cup warm water

2 glugs of honey

2 cups flour (I use a combination of white flour and oat flour)

1 cup oatmeal porridge (containing steel cut oats, oat flakes, quinoa and crushed flax seed)

1 egg

1 tbsp powdered gluten

1 tsp salt

Dissolve the yeast in the water and honey. Stir, cover and let stand for about 10 minutes.

In a warm bowl or mixer with a dough hook, combine the flour, oatmeal porridge, egg, gluten and salt. Add the yeast mixture and mix until the dough loses its stickiness. Let rise in the bowl for 1 hour, then shape and bake at 375 degrees for about 25 to 30 minutes.

Hot Cross Buns

My take on an Easter classic.

★ **Sometimes I also add dried cherries, chopped dried apricots and yellow raisins to my hot cross buns.**

2 packages active dry yeast

¼ cup milk, scalded

½ cup salad oil

⅓ cup sugar

Pinch of salt

3½ to 4 cups all-purpose flour

½ to 1 tsp ground cinnamon

A few good shakes of nutmeg

A few good shakes of allspice

3 eggs, beaten

⅔ cup dried currants

1 egg white, divided and slightly beaten

FROSTING

¾ cup icing sugar

¼ tsp vanilla

Dash of salt

Set the oven to 375 degrees. Soften the dry yeast in ½ cup warm water and set aside. Combine the milk, oil, sugar and salt, then cool to lukewarm.

Sift 1 cup of the flour with the spices and stir into the milk mixture. Add the eggs and beat well. Stir in the softened yeast and currants. Beat in the remaining flour, or enough to make a soft dough.

Cover the dough with a damp cloth and let rise in a warm place until its volume has doubled (about 1½ hours). Punch down the dough and turn out onto a lightly floured surface. Roll dough out to about ½ inch thickness. Cut with a floured 2½-inch round cutter and shape into buns.

Place the buns on a greased baking sheet, leaving enough space between for them to rise. Cover and let rise in a warm place until almost doubled in size (about 1 hour).

Cut shallow crosses in the tops of the buns with a very sharp knife. Brush the tops with some of the slightly beaten egg white (reserve the rest for something else). Bake for 15 minutes, then leave the buns out to cool slightly.

Mix the frosting ingredients together. Place it in a pastry tube, then pipe crosses onto the tops of each bun.

Pecan Bread

After a morning of shopping, my daughter Lisa and I went to a restaurant for lunch. We were seated at a table for four, but we were soon asked to move when a group of four came in. In appreciation for our giving up the table, the hostess served this bread with our meal. When we said how much we loved it, she gave us the recipe.

1 package instant yeast

½ cup warm water

1 tsp sugar

2 cups flour

¼ cup honey

2 tbsp oil

1½ tsp salt

1 large onion, slow-cooked in maple syrup

¾ cup to 1 cup toasted pecans

Dissolve the yeast in warm water and sugar. Mix all ingredients except the nuts and onions in a food processor or with a dough hook until it forms a smooth ball. Add nuts and onions and mix thoroughly.

Cover and let rise, then punch down and shape. Let rise again and bake at 375 degrees for about 25 minutes.

Muffins

I HAVE MADE EVERY KIND of muffin you can imagine—
some really great, others just okay. For many years, I would
get up, stumble into the kitchen and make a batch of muffins
without a recipe, and probably with one eye partially open. I
would toss them in the oven and begin my daily routine. Don
and I would each have a muffin for breakfast and the remaining
muffins would be packed off to Don's office for his staff.

Today, I enjoy getting up on Pender Island just as the sun is
rising and the sea is calm, going into our large island kitchen
and making muffins the way I used to—only now it is for hungry
holiday guests.

Over the years, I have developed a formula that works well
for me. I want my muffins to be as healthy as possible—full of
fruit, texture, moisture and intense flavour. Making great muffins
requires fresh products (organic when possible). To that end, I
generally use fruit in season or frozen berries. I also use a variety
of flours and sugars. I always chop and toast my nuts, then store
them in the refrigerator.

Some muffins are better with butter and others with oil. I try
to use unsalted organic butter and I vary my oil depending on
what is healthiest. When using milk, I either use organic whole
milk or buttermilk. For eggs, I use omega organic eggs. A food
processor is a must.

Pender Island Cornmeal Muffins

One rainy morning in the Gulf Islands, I made this version of cornmeal muffins. It has become a favourite, mostly because they seem less dry than other recipes. Everything here is approximate. I just don't measure when making muffins. But it is hard to go wrong with muffins—they tend to be very forgiving.

★ I have recently started adding about a half cup of mashed sweet potato to the wet ingredients. If you try this, you will likely need to add a bit more flour to keep the balance right.

1⅓ cup flour

⅔ cup cornmeal

⅔ cup almond flour

½ cup sugar

2 tsp baking powder

1 tsp baking soda

Pinch of salt

1 cup buttermilk

¼ cup melted butter

¼ cup sunflower oil

1 egg

1 tsp pure almond extract

1 cup berries (I like blueberries, saskatoon-berries, raspberries or a combination)

Mix together the dry ingredients and set aside. Mix together all of the wet ingredients except the berries. Mix the two together, then add the berries—do it quickly and don't over-beat the batter.

Place in muffin cups and bake at 350 degrees for about 20 minutes.

Carrot Muffins

TWO WAYS

These are both really good! The first way is an old favourite, and the second can be adapted for just about any fruit and nut combination.

★ For successful muffins you want to balance just the right amount of flour with the liquids, sugar and eggs. You also want to balance the fruit and the dough— add enough fruit to the dough so each muffin will have several pieces of fruit in it, but won't be overloaded.

FIRST WAY

2 cups flour

½ cup almond flour

¾ or more cups sugar, depending on how sweet you like your muffins

3 good shakes of cinnamon

3 good shakes of nutmeg

2 tsp baking powder

½ tsp baking soda

½ cups oil

2 tsp vanilla

3 eggs

⅓ cups buttermilk

4 medium/large carrots, grated

1 apple, peeled and chopped

8 pitted dates, chopped

A handful of raisins

½ cup chopped, toasted walnuts

Combine the dry ingredients first, then add the oil, vanilla, eggs and buttermilk. Mix very lightly. Add the carrot, fruit and walnuts and mix quickly, as little as possible. Place in paper-lined muffin tins and bake at 350 degrees until done (about 20 to 25 minutes).

SECOND WAY

2 cups flour

1 cup sugar (I use ½ brown and ½ white)

1½ tsp baking powder

1 tsp baking soda

2 tsp cinnamon

Pinch of allspice

Lots of freshly grated nutmeg
(probably about 2 tsp)

Pinch of salt

3 eggs

½ cup oil

About 1 tsp vanilla

3 large carrots, grated

1 apple, grated

½ cup pecans

½ cup raisins

About ¼ cup mixed pumpkin
and sunflower seeds

About 5 dried apricots, chopped

A small handful of dried cherries

Mix ingredients until just blended
(dry first, then add wet), then transfer
to muffin tins. The dough will be stiff.
Cook at about 350 degrees until done.
Check them at 20 minutes; because of
their density, they may require a little
more time.

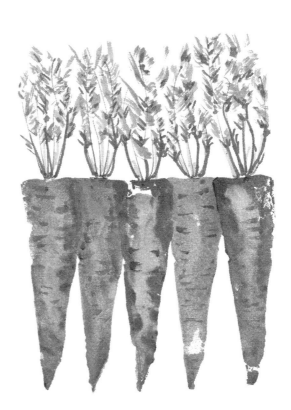

Pender Island Leftover Muffins

It is a rainy West Coast morning. The clouds hang low over the sea and it is time for breakfast, followed by packing and heading back to the mainland by ferry. My challenge is to use up all the leftover food and decide what goes and what stays. On this morning, the ingredients for my muffins include an orange, a banana and an apple. What results is probably one of the best muffin recipes I have ever made. Even Misha the dog loves these muffins.

1 orange

1 banana

1 egg and a dollop of egg white

Handful of oatmeal

1 lightly packed cup brown sugar

⅔ cup butter, or a combination of butter and oil

About ½ cup buttermilk

1 apple, chopped

Lots of nutmeg

Lots of cinnamon

White flour

Oat flour

About ½ tsp baking soda

2 heaping tbsp baking powder

Handful of dates

½ cup walnuts, chopped

Cut the orange into quarters, remove the seeds and put into a food processor. Then, one at a time, add the banana, egg and egg white, oatmeal, sugar, butter/oil and buttermilk. Blend thoroughly.

In a small bowl, combine the apple with nutmeg and cinnamon. Sprinkle with a little extra brown sugar.

In a large mixing bowl, combine the white flour and oat flour to total at least two cups—then have the flour handy, as you may need more. Add baking soda and baking powder and mix.

Toss some dates into the wet mixture after mixing, then combine all ingredients together except the walnuts. Move quickly and have your paper-lined muffin tins ready. The dough should be almost the consistency of a slightly loose cookie dough. Scoop the dough into the tins and top with chopped nuts. Bake at 350 degrees for about 20 to 25 minutes.

★ Keep your food processor on the counter. I use mine all the time.

Maggie and Paul's Best Muffins

1 orange

1 cup brown sugar

Cinnamon

Nutmeg

White flour

Oat flour

Almond flour

Baking powder

Baking soda

A good handful of dates, chopped

⅓ to ½ cup melted butter

3 eggs

2 glugs buttermilk

1 apple, chopped

Pecans, sugared, toasted and chopped

Finely chop the whole, unpeeled orange in a food processor. Set aside.

Mix the dry ingredients first, then fold in all of the wet ingredients, including the orange and the dates. Spoon into paper-lined muffin tins and top with pecans. Bake at 350 degrees for 12 to 15 minutes.

The best way to make good muffins is to learn the balance between wet and dry ingredients. You want the dough almost hard to mix—not watery. I never use amounts for this recipe, as this consistency is something you learn by feel. Practice and see for yourself— these muffins are really yummy!

Other Muffin Ideas

Here are a few types of muffins I routinely make. I cannot share exact recipes because I never do it exactly the same way twice. I never measure anything. I do it by feel and by how it appears as I go along. If you like, you can try adapting the second way of the Carrot Muffins (page 31) to make any these.

★ **You can freeze bananas to use later in baking or shakes.**

Almond and Cherry Use natural almond flavouring and toasted almonds.

Apple/Cinnamon/Nutmeg With pecans.

Banana with Walnuts And anything else, or nothing else!

Bran Remember, molasses is great with bran.

Cornmeal Plain or with berries such as saskatoonberries, blueberries or raspberries.

Lemon/Blueberry and Blackberry Always use fresh lemon rind.

Mixed Berries In season, with lemon.

Orange/Date and Pecans I always pop the whole orange in the food processor, so it generally makes up most of the liquid. Remember to keep a balance between wet and dry.

Peach In season, with raspberries.

Poppy Seed/Lemon A tasty combination.

Pumpkin Plain or with dates, apples or sometimes chocolate chips. I often use leftover winter squash the same way I use pumpkin.

Sometimes, I also put different toppings on my muffins. Here are a few options:

- A crumble mix, much like what you would use for a crisp—butter, sugar, flour, oatmeal, vanilla, cinnamon and nutmeg. I might also add nuts to this mixture.

- After they are baked, apply warm golden corn syrup (heated in the microwave) to the tops of the muffins while they are still hot. I sometimes mix a little cinnamon and nutmeg into the corn syrup before applying to the muffins.

- For cornmeal muffins, I sometimes warm a little maple butter (the stuff you buy in a jar) just to soften it, then drizzle it on top of the warm muffins.

These are just a few ideas. Enjoy!

Scones

Scones are so easy to make—you just have to keep some of what I call my "Master Mix" on hand. Just scoop what you think you will need of the mix into the food processor and add what you choose—some of my favourite combinations follow.

Master Mix (page 267)

1 egg

Milk or water

Flavour or filling of your choice
(see suggestions below)

Put some Master Mix in the food processor and add an egg and enough milk or water to create the right consistency. Add your flavourings, then mix a little bit longer.

Form your scones, plop them straight onto the baking pan and bake at 375 degrees for about 12 minutes in a steam oven set at about 30% steam, or in a regular oven at 375 to 400 degrees for 10 to 15 minutes. All ovens are different—just pay attention and adjust the heat and time as needed.

Currant and Lemon Add lemon rind, yogurt and currants.

Goat Cheese and Onion Add two green onions, finely chopped. Choose a really good feta and buttermilk.

Orange and Cranberry This is Lisa's recipe. Add a drop or two of orange oil, orange rind and cranberries.

Pumpkin Add pumpkin purée from a can. It has a lot of moisture, so go easy on the buttermilk and add one egg. Process, bake and, when the scones are done, drizzle maple butter on them.

★ **This tip comes from our friend Leigh-Anne: when making scones, grate cold or frozen butter into the flour. This improves the end product.**

Doris McCarthy

DORIS MCCARTHY, ninety-four, studied under Arthur Lismer, one of the Group of Seven. Doris is regarded as one of Canada's finest artists. I am listening to her being interviewed by Shelagh Rogers on CBC's *Sounds Like Canada*.

Tuning in to the interview, I am aware that there are very few intrusions I would allow into this space—my "alone time," when I quietly dismantle our Christmas tree. It is my ritual to carefully, lovingly bring closure to the festive season and prepare for a New Year with new hopes and dreams.

Doris, whom I met several years ago, is a welcome guest in our living room on this chilly December day. She is describing the rich fibre of her life. I resonate with her joy, holding each precious ornament—a library of my life.

My disassembling begins at the bottom of the tree. The task is long, for I stop many times to reminisce.

First is the head of a Santa, with his bright blue button eyes giving me a glassy stare, glued on a stocking face that's partly covered in cotton batting. I remember when my child proudly presented the Santa head to be placed on our family tree. That child, now an adult, is a social worker in a large hospital.

There is a stained glass church we bought in Hawaii when the children were small.

The glass teardrops from WM Heard's studio in Vancouver, purchased years ago with my friend Marion.

Pearlized green balls. A gift from daughter Suzanne to Don to welcome him into our family.

Doris McCarthy explains how colours and shapes fascinate her. Listening, I caress the oldest ornament, the one from my earliest childhood. I remember Dad bringing it home. A large, very delicate shiny red ball with gold stardust swirling around it, creating a magical pattern.

Next, a golden pear. So smooth to the touch, and holding a rich depth of colour. It was a gift from Lisa a few years ago.

I stand between our trees, a white spruce from our land outside the city, at the other end of the room. On the wall behind me hangs a painting by McCarthy, called *The Cedars*.

All memories on the tree are not happy. Some bring sorrow. I remove the soft white crocheted snowman. A gift from a friend passed. We lost touch along the way. Busy lives often take different directions. She died of breast cancer a few months ago.

A smaller golden pear floods my thoughts with the Christmas my mother died. The children bought the mirrored pear in the gift shop of the hospital, to remember Gramma.

A rich green ribbon loops around a strong branch of the spruce. It is the ribbon Seka, our dog, wore last Christmas, just before she died. Beside it, a crystal heart in memory of our other deceased dog, Ty, a gift from one of his caregivers.

Looking over at *The Cedars*, I return to the May day I bought the painting for Don's birthday. It certainly was a financial stretch, but he'd seen it and loved it. I went to the Scott Gallery alone and stood in front of it for a very long time, finally handing over my credit card. I vowed no new clothes for a while. The painting remained on display in the gallery while Don and I went to Toronto for a business trip. During the trip we celebrated his birthday. At dinner, I presented him with a card saying "Happy Birthday." He looked confused. "No present?" As he opened the card, a photo of *The Cedars* fluttered to the table. The look on his face was worth no new clothes.

At the top of our Christmas tree is the angel who has presided over many celebrations. Her wings have been glued on after many falls. Her colours have faded with time. Still, her ethereal presence represents a higher order, pulling out the good in all of us, casting away fear, freeing us to explore our creative lives.

As the interview draws to a close, Shelagh asks Doris about aging. "It is great. I love getting older. I can do anything I want. I am free," explains Doris. "What about ice skating? You love it?" Shelagh asks.

"I had a fall two years ago. My balance is a bit off and no, I cannot ice skate anymore. Today, I skate in my mind. Just close my eyes. I feel the chill on my face as I twirl around the rink. Yes, I am really very happy!" says Doris.

My Best Biscuits

These biscuits really are fabulous—
light and moist, with great texture. If
you wish, you can add dried fruit and
decrease the sugar slightly.

1⅔ to 2 cups flour

Pinch of kosher salt

1 tbsp baking powder, plus an extra pinch

¾ tsp baking soda

⅓ to ½ cup butter, cold

1 egg

1 cup buttermilk

Put less than 2 cups of flour in a food
processor. Add the salt, baking powder
and baking soda.

Chop the cold butter into chunks and add,
then process the mixture until the butter is
about the size of very small peas.

Place the egg in a 1-cup measure and add
buttermilk to just past the 1-cup mark. Pour
the wet mixture over the flour mixture and
process until blended. The mixture should
be fairly stiff.

Scoop it out with a spoon into a well-
greased pie pan. The biscuits will just be
blobs—they should hold their shape. Bake
at 375 degrees for about 10 minutes, then
lower the temperature to about 350 degrees
to finish them off—probably about 12 more
minutes, but keep checking on them.

★ Don't be afraid to use more baking
   powder than a recipe calls for. I find it
   makes a better product.

Popovers

We were first served popovers with a lovely chicken salad in Hawaii. These are baked in popover tins, similar to Yorkshire puddings.

★ I now buy full fat for all dairy products. I feel it is healthier.

2 eggs

1 cup milk

2 tbsp melted butter

1 cup flour

½ tsp salt

Mix all of the ingredients and let rest for 30 minutes. Preheat oven to 425 degrees. Pour mixture into warmed tins that are well-coated with grapeseed oil.

Put the popovers in the oven and lower the temperature to between 350 and 375 degrees. Bake for about 20 to 30 minutes. When golden brown, remove and serve promptly.

Cottage Crêpes

When we are at our Gulf Island cottage and I get tired of eggs, I make crêpes. The base for this sauce is the same—add whatever fruit you wish. I have used bananas, mangos, strawberries, peaches, pineapple or oranges, alone or in any combination.

★ Crêpes are wonderful with a combination of plums, cherries, sugar, vanilla and a pinch of powdered star anise. Or, mix orange juice with a little cornstarch and sugar, then add orange segments, mango and pineapple. Toss in a sliced banana, if you wish.

1¼ cups flour

3 eggs, lightly beaten, plus 1 egg white

1 cup milk

3 tbsp sugar

2 tbsp melted butter

Rind from about half a lemon

Pinch of salt

SAUCE

2 tsp butter

¼ cup brown sugar

Juice of one or more oranges

Rind from about half the orange

Fruit of your choice—anything organic and in-season

Place all of the crêpe ingredients in a food processor and blend. Set aside in the fridge.

Melt butter in frying pan, then add all of the sauce ingredients. Gently simmer.

While sauce is simmering, fry crêpes in a nonstick frying pan. Serve with your favourite fruit sauce, along with either some whipping cream or a dollop of Blin (page 17).

Milk with Cream on Top

WHEN WE ARE IN the city, breakfast is usually an efficient meal, consisting of porridge or simple eggs. But on Pender Island, breakfast is an event; we pull out all the stops, serving lattes, coffee and a really big meal with eggs, pancakes or waffles, bacon, ham and lots of fresh fruit, followed with more lattes, coffee, muffins and visiting. After breakfast and visiting often comes serious gardening, along with cutting wood for the open fireplace in the great room or the pizza oven. These activities are followed with a hike up Mount Menzies, or maybe some crabbing or boating.

Because we use a lot of milk for lattes and porridge we are very particular about what milk we purchase. One day, standing in front of the milk cooler, I am reaching for our favourite local, organic grass-fed milk when suddenly a voice beside us speaks up: "Good choice." We engage in a long conversation with the man beside us—apparently, he has been involved in milk research, and the story we hear from him is this: buy grass-fed, organic milk with cream on top. It turns out what we should be drinking is what our mothers used before milk was modified.

Pancakes

This is my favourite pancake recipe. I even like these cold. They remind me of Mrs. Dunlop's doughnuts. Mrs. Dunlop was our neighbour when I was a child, and every week she made a batch of cake doughnuts and often shared them with us—a major treat! The banana provides moisture and you can hardly taste it.

★ Always use real vanilla when you cook, and be generous with it.

1 cup white flour

⅔ cup oat flour

⅔ cup almond flour

⅔ cup quinoa flour

2 tbsp baking powder

¼ cup cold butter, cut into chunks

1 tsp freshly grated nutmeg

1 banana, mashed

⅛ cup sugar

2 cups buttermilk

4 eggs, plus an optional dollop of additional egg white

1 tbsp pure vanilla

Place the flours, baking powder, butter and nutmeg in a food processor and blend. Remove contents, place in a large bowl and set aside.

Mash a banana and place in the food processor with the sugar, buttermilk, eggs and vanilla. Mix until completely smooth, then combine with the dry ingredients. Do not overmix.

Drop in spoonfuls on a hot griddle to cook.

Waffles

TWO WAYS

I am a waffle junkie. After having really good waffles while travelling, I have tried to perfect them at home. It has been a long, difficult journey, but here are two methods I love. The first is a classic waffle, and the second is my current favourite!

FIRST WAY

2 cups flour

½ cup dry buttermilk

2 tbsp sugar

2 tsp baking powder

½ tsp baking soda

⅓ cup cold butter, cut into small pieces

3 eggs, separated

¼ tsp cream of tartar

About 1 cup buttermilk

2 large spoonfuls sour cream

Some grated lemon rind or 1 tsp vanilla

Mix the first 5 ingredients in the food processor. Add butter and process until the butter is mixed in and is in very small bits.

Beat the egg whites with cream of tartar until stiff and set aside. Mix the egg yolks with buttermilk, sour cream and grated lemon rind or vanilla.

In a large bowl, combine the dry ingredients with the egg yolk mixture, then quickly fold in the stiff egg whites. Do not overmix. Place in a very hot iron and cook until golden. After cooking, let waffles rest in the oven at 200 degrees for 2 minutes.

SECOND WAY

1½ cups flour

½ cup almond flour

¼ cup cornstarch

Salt

Baking powder and baking soda

2 tbsp sugar

Nutmeg

1½ cups buttermilk

½ cup milk

7 tbsp oil

4 eggs, separated

Vanilla

Mix dry ingredients and set aside. Mix all wet ingredients except the egg whites (you can add the yolks in now, though) and incorporate into the dry ingredients. Whip egg whites to a stiff consistency and fold in. Cook in your waffle iron.

★ To make a good waffle, you need heat, so if you are planning to get a waffle iron, find out what the wattage is. Most of those on the market really aren't that good. They produce a soggy, soft, light-brown waffle that just doesn't cut it with me. However, I have now found a waffle iron that I like at Williams-Sonoma—an All-Clad Belgian waffle maker that cooks four at a time.

Eggs Benny Our Way

There are many ways to do eggs Benedict. We like this one, developed after many good breakfasts at a seaside bistro in Vancouver—it uses soft cheese in place of tricky hollandaise sauce. If you are serving these eggs to a group, you can do a lot of the prep the night before and stick the bread bases in the fridge. Pop them in the oven the next morning and you are set. Even the eggs can be partially poached and held in the fridge.

Eggs

Focaccia

Sun-dried tomato butter

Basil

Ham

Gruyere, brie, fontina or meltable cheese of your choice

Cut a piece of focaccia in half widthwise and lightly toast it. Lace the sun-dried tomato butter with basil and spread it over the bread. Top with a slice of good ham. Top that with a tangy, soft cheese that you might like with eggs (I use cave-aged gruyere or fontina).

Warm the bread bases in the oven. Top with poached eggs, then cover the whole thing with more cheese (or, if you prefer, with hollandaise, served on top or on the side).

Grilled Tomatoes
TWO WAYS

When Don and I were in Italy, we had grilled tomatoes every morning with our poached eggs. Here is my recipe (the first way), followed by Don's (the second way).

FIRST WAY

12 cherry tomatoes

A handful of fresh oregano, chopped

Pinch of kosher salt

Olive oil

Sauté the tomatoes in oil and top with the oregano and salt. Serve with breakfast.

SECOND WAY

4 tomatoes, sliced

Oregano

Garlic powder

Thyme

Olive oil or bacon grease

Top the tomato slices with oregano, garlic powder and thyme. Slow cook in a skillet in a little olive oil or bacon grease for about 1 hour.

Italian Breakfast Tomatoes

We first had these in Florence, served with our poached eggs. The tomatoes arrived hot in a skillet as a side to our eggs and toast. We like these with HP Sauce.

★ **These tomatoes can be served immediately, or frozen.**

Several handfuls of cherry tomatoes

Oregano

Salt and pepper

Garlic powder

Grapeseed oil or virgin olive oil

Fresh basil (if you have some)

Place the tomatoes in a hot pan that has been warmed with grapeseed oil. Sprinkle oregano, salt, pepper and garlic powder overtop while quickly shaking the pan. Serve when the skins start to wither slightly, and top with fresh basil.

Appetizers and Tapas

Bruschetta

I love bruschetta, but it is messy to eat so I only serve it as an appie if we are sitting at a table.

3 tomatoes, chopped

¾ cup basil

Sweet onion, chopped

A couple cloves of garlic, chopped
(a mix of fresh and roasted is good)

Small amount of olive oil

Splash of good-quality balsamic vinegar

Toast or sliced baguette

Goat cheese

Mix the tomatoes, basil, onion and garlic and toss with a little olive oil and balsamic. Spoon onto freshly toasted bread and top with a dollop of goat cheese. Broil in the oven until the cheese is melted.

★ **As an alternative, try making bruschetta with a mix of canned butter beans, garlic, lemon juice and olive oil. Mix it all up in a food processor and top on toast with crisp prosciutto.**

Cheese Crisps

Our friend and writing partner Mufty shared this wonderful recipe with us.

1 package soft Imperial cheese

½ cup oil

½ tbsp Worcestershire sauce

1 tsp salt

1 cup flour

2 cups Rice Krispies

3 dashes Tabasco sauce (a must!)

Mix all of the ingredients and place in small mounds on an ungreased baking sheet. Flatten with a fork.

Bake at 350 degrees for about 10 to 12 minutes. Watch them carefully so they don't burn.

Toasted Marcona Almonds

Marcona almonds can be hard to find but the search is worth it. I buy mine at Superstore or Whole Foods.

Marcona almonds

Truffle oil

Maldon or sea salt

★ **Be careful! More than once when roasting nuts I have set them on fire.**

Toast a handful of Marcona almonds in a frying pan, then roll them sparingly in a little truffle oil. Top with sea salt. Yum!

Dates and Prosciutto

A version of this wonderful appie is served at a lovely restaurant in Calgary.

Good Medjool dates

Walnuts, toasted

Prosciutto, thinly sliced

Maldon or sea salt

Balsamic vinegar

Make an opening in the date and remove the pit. Place one large toasted walnut in the centre. Wrap in prosciutto and warm.

Serve warm with salt and a good balsamic vinegar.

★ **I recently served this as an appetizer for a lamb tagine; for that, I stuffed a soft cheese in the dates along with the walnut. It was really nice!**

Spring Rolls

These make for tasty and crispy appetizers!

★ **To make these spring rolls even easier, just buy pre-made sweet chili sauce for dipping.**

Sauté garlic and ginger in a pan with peanut oil. Add the carrots, cabbage, water chestnuts, cayenne and chicken and cook. Allow to cool, then add mint, basil and cilantro.

Place about 1 good tbsp of the mixture into each wrapper. Fry in grapeseed oil till golden. Serve with dipping sauce.

Spring roll wrappers

Peanut oil

Garlic, to taste

Ginger, to taste

Carrots and cabbage, thinly sliced

Water chestnuts, chopped

½ tsp cayenne

Shredded, cooked chicken (optional)

Mint

Basil

Cilantro

Grapeseed oil, for frying

DIPPING SAUCE

2 tbsp soy sauce

2 tsp fish sauce

2 tsp lime juice

1 tbsp sugar

Asparagus Rolls

Our friend Patricia serves these in a tall glass before dinner.

Asparagus spears, ends trimmed off

Herbed cream cheese

Prosciutto (thinly sliced)

Steam the asparagus to al dente. Coat the prosciutto with cream cheese, then wrap it around the asparagus. Chill, then serve upright in a drinking glass.

Toast Crisps

This appie recipe comes from my friend Marion. It can be done ahead, is easily transported and can be made well before dinner. Present using a large, beautiful tray or serving platter with the toasts spread out. Use parsley or another garnish of your choice.

1 French baguette

Butter

Camembert, or any soft, spreadable cheese

Topping of your choice

Thinly slice a good French baguette and butter the pieces on one side. Place on a cookie sheet, buttered side up. Bake at about 300 degrees until golden and crisp. Cool and store in an air-tight container until ready to use.

To serve, spread the crisps with soft cheese and a topping of your choice. Options include any pâté or cheese topped with Tomato Jam (page 256); dates and walnuts with Maldon salt and balsamic; fava beans topped with chives or black olives; or goat cheese and cherry tomatoes with fresh basil.

★ **Just about any topping works for this— let your imagination roll!**

Warm Crabmeat Dip

A delicious, luxurious appetizer.

1 cup fresh crab

3 hardboiled eggs, mashed

½ cup mayonnaise

1 tbsp grated onion

½ tsp salt

Pinch of white pepper

Dash of cayenne pepper

1 cup water chestnuts, chopped

1½ cup bread crumbs

2 tbsp butter, melted

Parsley, chopped

Freshly grated Parmesan cheese

Mix all of the ingredients together except the bread crumbs, butter, parsley and cheese. Let mixture stand overnight.

Mix the bread crumbs with melted butter and some chopped parsley. Combine with the crab mixture, place in a greased pan and sprinkle with Parmesan cheese. Bake at 325 degrees until warmed through.

Garlic Bread

I have made this garlic bread for years, and we even served it at my daughter Lisa's wedding. I use it for almost all dinner parties involving steaks or beef of any kind. It is also great with ribs.

★ If you only have supermarket bread, save your energy for something else. The bread must be the best you can get. The loaf I choose is crispy on the outside and flavourful and chewy inside.

Good French bread

1 lb butter, soft but not melted

Fresh garlic, at least one good-sized head

Garlic powder

⅓ cup or more of really good-quality, freshly grated Parmesan

Chives, finely chopped

Parsley, finely chopped

Cut the bread into 1-inch slices. Mix all of the remaining ingredients together and spread generously on the sliced bread. You can wrap and freeze the loaf or set it aside; just warm it thoroughly in the oven before serving. To heat, wrap in tinfoil and place in the oven at 325 to 350 degrees for about 15 minutes, or a bit longer if you are heating from frozen.

COVID Magic

EVEN DURING COVID, good can happen. Don and I have made a temporary move to Calgary during this time to be near his work and our children.

It has been heartbreaking for me to see the poverty and difficult times in this lovely province. After years of prosperity, Alberta is truly in trouble.

Thanksgiving is different in October 2020. Our small family gathers masked, with clean hands re-washed upon entering. With great caution, we meet to celebrate our love and friendship. As we share appies, a cell pings: a text has arrived from the most easterly part of Canada. It reads:

Me and my family wish you and your family and friends all the love in the world. Your kindness will always be remembered. Our prayers will be with you forever. We are so happy.

A very grateful mother.

Our daughter, a tall, lovely blond woman, re-reads the text she has just received. She has been an advocate for a young woman and her family, and, after weeks of frustrating attempts to reunite them, a magic end has finally come.

The young woman came to Alberta to work, and, through no fault of her own, became ill. Her medical issues created significant financial problems along with the physical ones—leaving her without funds and completely helpless. She faced a cruel destiny: having her beloved cat put down, and being placed in a long-term care facility somewhere here in Alberta.

It seemed like she had no way to manage a safe return home. All doors were closed. *But this can't be true*, I thought when I first heard the story. I remember saying out loud: "I cannot live in a society that does not have an answer to this problem."

At the same time I was having this thought, the magic was already starting to do its work. A caring and compassionate community stepped forward to help, under the guidance of a competent advocate—my daughter. A church with a strong mandate for social justice, a first-class airline, an off-duty paramedic, a retired nurse and a cluster of other folks all did their part. Treats were purchased, along with a cat carrier and duffel bags for a long journey back across the continent that would finally end in Atlantic Canada.

Now, the young woman has arrived safely home into the loving arms of her family. And as we begin our own Thanksgiving meal, a precocious six-year-old playing with his carrots belts out, "Good job, Auntie!"

Quick Shrimp Pâté

This is really good and fast! Basically, all you need is a bag of small frozen shrimp. The other ingredients are things you probably have on hand, and substitution works.

★ **If you don't have ketchup, lemon juice or horseradish, you can just buy a package of red shrimp cocktail sauce and use that instead.**

Frozen cooked shrimp

Ketchup

Lemon juice

Horseradish

Mayonnaise

Chopped chives

Hot sauce (a small amount)

Cream cheese

Dump as many frozen shrimp as you want in the food processor, then add the remaining ingredients to taste and process. Place mixture in a bowl and refrigerate until ready to serve. I usually serve it with my own Toast Crisps (page 53).

Smoked Salmon Rolls

These rolls are easy to make and easy to eat. They retain their shape, making them good "stand-up" food.

Smoked salmon

Several large soft tortilla shells

Cream cheese mixed with a little goat cheese

Dill

Capers

Parsley (for garnish)

Spread the cheese on the tortillas and top with dill and smoked salmon. Sprinkle capers over the salmon and roll up like a jelly roll. Wrap in plastic wrap and refrigerate until ready to use. Slice the rolls in bite-sized pieces and place on a tray decorated with parsley.

Salmon Mousse

This recipe can be made a day ahead, and can easily be doubled for a larger gathering. I often put it in an interesting bowl with capers scattered on top and surround it with crackers or dried toast.

★ This mixture can be placed in a fancy mould, then unmoulded onto lettuce and decorated with lemon wedges and capers.

¼ cup cold water

1 package unflavoured gelatin

1 tin of good-quality red salmon (remove the skin and bones)

½ cup mayonnaise

Green onion, finely chopped

A splash of Tabasco sauce

1 tbsp lemon juice

1 heaping tsp horseradish

½ cup whipping cream, whipped

Dissolve the gelatin in the cold water. Add all of the remaining ingredients except the whipping cream. Mix, then fold in the cream. Chill until set.

Lamb Samosas

TWO WAYS

These can be used as an appie or served with a salad for lunch. The second way is a little spicier and uses spring roll wrappers instead of filo pastry.

★ **Always remove and discard the centre of fresh garlic—it can be very bitter.**

FIRST WAY

Ground lamb

Filo pastry

1 cup diced potatoes

1 cup peas

Onion, finely chopped

Garlic

Pistachios, shelled, toasted and chopped

Coriander

Turmeric

Powdered or fresh ginger

Cardamom

Fennel seeds

Pepper

Fresh mint

Melted butter

Cook the potato and peas and set aside. Meanwhile, sauté the lamb with the remaining ingredients, save for the filo, mint and melted butter. Once cooked, add the potatoes, peas and mint.

Make triangles of the filo, then place half of the triangles on parchment paper on a baking sheet. Place a spoonful of the mixture on each triangle and top with the reserved filo. Brush them with butter and bake at about 400 degrees for 15 minutes, until golden.

Serve with a good chutney.

SECOND WAY

4 lamb sausages

Spring roll wrappers

Red onions, finely chopped

Fresh ginger, grated

Garlic

Fresh mint

Nuts of your choice, chopped

Coriander

Cinnamon

Cumin

Cardamom

1 tbsp celery, finely chopped

1 small yam, finely chopped

1 tbsp yellow pepper, finely chopped

½ beaten egg (optional, to help with binding)

Cook the lamb sausages and break up the meat. Sauté the cooked lamb with the remaining filling ingredients. Spoon the lamb into the wrappers and either bake as in the first way or fry in oil to a light golden brown.

Serve with either a sweet chili dipping sauce or a good chutney.

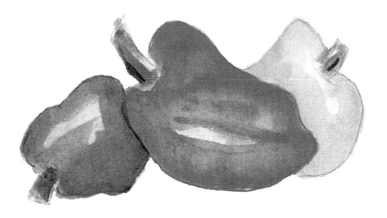

Soups

Beet Watermelon Soup

If you want to try a really good summer soup, this is it! I made it by accident one hot day in Vancouver, and I just love it. These were the ingredients I had, so I just went ahead and made a soup. Use your own judgement—most amounts are approximate.

4 medium-sized beets, peeled and chopped

1 onion, chopped

2 cloves garlic, peeled and chopped

4 cups watermelon, chopped and seeded

Juice of 1 orange

Juice of ½ lime

Sauté the beets, onion and garlic in a little oil, then cover with a small amount of water to finish cooking. When cooked and cooled, process with the remaining ingredients in a food processor.

Chill and enjoy!

Joyce's Watermelon Gazpacho Soup

I am part of a wonderful writing group in Edmonton. At a recent gathering, our fellow group member Joyce brought this soup. Everyone loved it! She has kindly shared it with me, but, like me, she does not measure.

Cranberry juice

1 small watermelon, cut into medium-size chunks with seeds removed

1 cucumber, chopped

Celery, chopped

Red and green peppers, chopped

Mint, sliced in fine strips ("chiffonade")

Red onion, chopped

Parsley, chopped

Lime juice

Sherry vinegar

1 jalapeño, finely chopped, without the seeds

Mix, chill and serve. Top with crumbled feta.

Carrot Mango Soup

This soup is good either hot or cold, but I generally serve it cold. It's great to serve in a demitasse before dinner. Place a small cracker or biscuit on the side.

★ I always buy organic, low-sodium chicken stock in Tetra Paks.

6 large carrots, chopped

1 sweet onion, chopped

1 tsp curry powder

1 tsp cumin

1 to 2 L chicken stock

1 tbsp lemon or lime juice

2 or 3 mangos, peeled and chopped

Sauté the carrots, onion, curry and cumin in a small amount of oil. When partially cooked, cover with the stock, add the lemon juice and cook until the veggies are tender.

When the mixture is cool, process in the blender with the mango. If necessary, add more stock, then put in the refrigerator until ready to use. Garnish with fresh parsley. If you are not planning to use the soup within a day or two, freeze it for later use.

Our Patron and Park Protector

I **WONDER—CAN ONE** woman so profoundly impact the culture of our little park community? The answer is yes! For she is its pulse, preserver and defender. With her watchful eye, dauntless force and endless spirit, she connects all living things in this tiny bustling park.

The first time I spot her, it is the day after a heavy rainfall. She is bent over, picking up earthworms with a twig and returning them gently back onto the wet grass, with her constant and patient companion, a small white fluffy dog, at her side. I ask, "What are you doing?" and she replies, "Taking the worms off the cement walkway before they get dehydrated and die."

And so, after every heavy rainfall, you will see her in the park: red jacket, brown curly hair, dog at her side, respectfully returning the earthworms to their natural habitat.

One cold and windy day, we are chatting briefly in the park when along comes a girl on crutches, her coat open and flying in the cruel wind, her scarf askew. She shivers with cold as our park protector approaches her. "Let me button your coat and fix your scarf." She begins the task, not waiting for an answer. The grateful girl thanks her and hobbles off into the storm, intact. I stand transfixed by my neighbour's keen observation skills and simple act of kindness.

Now it is 2007, and Vancouver is in the middle of a long and tedious civic strike, meaning no garbage pickup and no lawn or park service. The grass is almost knee-deep and the stench of garbage overflowing from bins hangs heavy over our park. As I enter the park I see her once again bent over in the long grass, with her faithful dog next to her. She appears to be looking for something. She sees me, straightens up and explains, "It's cutlery I am looking for—you know, the good stuff they sell at Puddifoot up in Kerrisdale."

Sure, I know Puddifoot, but what is cutlery doing in the long grass in the park? Apparently, for several weeks, late at night, someone has been coming into the park and dropping cutlery around in the grass, but only bits and pieces. So every morning our friend and neighbour gets up early and goes searching for whatever might be left from the night before. Our park protector proudly announces she almost has a sixteen-piece set.

Later, with determination, vision and perseverance, our park protector conceives and creates a group called Divas, a collection of women from all walks of life brought together for lunch on the first Friday of every month. Being mindful of the ladies' varying financial circumstances and wanting the lunch to be accessible to all, she suggests inexpensive and cheerful venues.

Our park protector makes it her job to invite any and all women she has been seeing daily in the park. She encourages present members to bring friends or visiting relatives along. If you are new to the "hood" you will be invited. If you are lonely, you will be scooped up and brought along to be introduced to new friends. Her inclusiveness and all-embracing behaviour is far-reaching and makes all feel welcome. One Diva takes a number of buses from about forty kilometres away just to "hang" with the ladies once a month.

The park protector—our Head Diva—has been known to boss us all around, with spunk and sparkle—strangely, it's not offensive but kind of sweet and caring. She certainly has earned the right to be in charge. With tenacity and dedication, year in and year out, she has never missed a lunch. She keeps the Divas connected and directed, pretty much knowing every move made by all of us. She is truly a powerful force with a golden heart.

I remember the psalm "To everything there is a season." Winter fades as spring approaches. Early one morning I am sitting at my desk, coffee in hand, looking out over our tiny park deep in thought. For all of us, different friends bring various lessons and gifts. The gifts given to me by our park protector are far-reaching. Besides helping me feel welcome in my new home and introducing me to new friends, she has also helped me learn to be more open and

"West Coast" in my approach to life—casual and relaxed in everything, so unlike my Prairie roots. I hold these precious gifts close and will always be grateful.

All is quiet as a small ray of sun shines through the trees. A gentle mist blankets the entire park after a heavy rain. The shiny green trees glisten with morning dew.

My gaze roams the park and suddenly I see her, stooped over, twig in hand, red jacket, curly brown hair and faithful dog by her side. She's carefully placing the earthworms back in the grass. As I blink, she vanishes, leaving only a calm and immense silence and a void in the social fibre of our tiny park. For our park protector has passed on.

And again, like our park, "To everything there is a season."

Cream of Broccoli Soup

This soup freezes very well.

Garlic butter

2 potatoes, chopped

5 celery stalks, chopped

6 leeks, chopped

1 onion, chopped

2 large heads broccoli, stems and
top divided, chopped

Fresh pepper

Steak salt

Tarragon (shallot tarragon is best)

Your favourite all-purpose spice blend

Thyme

Summer savory

1 bunch Swiss chard, chopped

1 bunch spinach, chopped

200 grams cheddar cheese, grated

½ tub mascarpone

Sauté the potatoes, celery, leeks and
onion in garlic butter. Add the broccoli
stems and continue cooking till al dente.
Add the spices, then add the chard, spinach
and the rest of the chopped broccoli.

Simmer until cooked, then add cheeses.
Blend until smooth, then serve!

★ **When freezing soups or stews, freeze
them flat in a resealable plastic bag with
a "best before" label on it.**

Kohlrabi Soup

I love kohlrabi soup! It is easy to make and freezes well.

★ If you wish, you can use the green kohlrabi tops as well, so long as they are young and in good condition.

4 medium-sized kohlrabi

1 sweet onion

1 large carrot

2 stalks celery

1 clove garlic

Butter

1 L chicken stock

Pinch of salt

¼ tsp tarragon leaves, crushed

Handful of fresh parsley

Milk as necessary, usually about 1 cup (try to use organic)

Chop the veggies and sauté them in a little butter. When al dente, add chicken stock and cook until tender. Add milk and the salt and herbs to taste.

When cool, blend in batches, then freeze in containers or store in the fridge. Serve hot.

Fennel Pear Soup

This is also a good bet for serving prior to dinner in a demitasse.

★ Soak cut pears in a solution of ascorbic acid to keep them white.

Butter

3 good-sized fennel bulbs, chopped

4 leeks, chopped

1 small potato, peeled and chopped

1 to 2 L chicken stock

3 pears, peeled and chopped

2 tbsp cream

Chopped parsley, chives and peppercress

Sauté the veggies in a little butter until al dente, then cover with the stock and finish cooking. When cool, add pears and cream, then process with a blender. Top with parsley, chives and peppercress.

The Farmers' Market

ON A BEAUTIFUL SUNNY Vancouver day, I head to Granville Island. Every Thursday in summer, they have an outdoor farmers' market right beside the main market. Farmers come in from the Fraser Valley with wonderful local organic produce and flowers. Even though we live very close to the market, on Thursdays I always take the car. I come home loaded with wonderful goodies—too many to carry on foot!

It is 8 a.m. and the outdoor market doesn't officially open until 9 a.m., but sales are brisk. My first stop is the tomato man. He has organic romas and other wonderful heritage varieties, freshly picked. His tomatoes will never see the inside of a supermarket. I purchase two large bags of romas—today is soup day!

Next, it is treat time for my breakfast, which I have yet to eat. I stop at Beckmann's, my favourite place for blueberries, strawberries and raspberries. Today they have blueberries in two varieties, large early ones and a smaller later variety, as well as strawberries that are red throughout (not those white-centred hard things). These berries have not been sprayed. The woman ahead of me asks: "Which blueberries are best?" Mrs. Beckmann says: "Try one of each—you choose." She takes the early variety and so do I. I am amazed at the flavour of the berries—so intense, sweet and huge, almost the size of a small cherry. This fruit will go well with my cottage cheese and organic yogurt.

Inside the market, I purchase an organic fair-trade latte and a piece of grape, walnut and pine nut bread. With bags stuffed to the overflow point and balancing my latte carefully, I head to the car and home. But not before giving myself a moment to feel how very fortunate I am to be here in such a food heaven beside the sea.

Pear and Parsnip Soup

This soup is smooth and delicious.

Butter

1 clove garlic, minced or pressed

1 organic red pepper, chopped

3 pears, peeled and chopped

5 good-sized parsnips, peeled, cored and chopped

1½ L chicken stock

Melt some butter in pot. Add veggies and pears and sauté. Add stock, cook till soft and purée. Serve hot.

Really Good Asparagus Soup

This is another soup that freezes well. You will need two pots to make this one.

Lots of fresh asparagus, chopped (hard base and soft green parts divided)

Leeks, chopped (white and green parts divided)

Shallots, finely chopped

Carrots, chopped

3 tbsp mashed potatoes

Spinach, chopped

Whipping cream

Crème fraiche

Place chopped shallots, carrots, the hard bases of the asparagus and the white parts of the leeks in a pot and add about 1½ cups of water. Let simmer into a stock.

In a second pot, add mashed potatoes, the green parts of the leek and asparagus and the spinach, and gently cook in a small amount of the stock. Do not overcook!

Strain the stock from the first pot and pour into the second pot. Remove from the heat and add whipping cream and crème fraiche. Purée till blended.

Roasted Apple and Squash Soup

This is great served before supper in demitasses. It's also wonderful with grilled cheese sandwiches.

1 or 2 large butternut squashes, peeled, seeded and cut into chunks

2 large, flavourful apples, peeled and cut into quarters

1 celeriac, peeled and chopped

2 stalks celery, chopped

2 carrots, chopped

Brown sugar

1½ cups apple juice

1 L chicken stock

A pinch of thyme

½ cup mascarpone

Toss the veggies and apples in a little olive oil and brown sugar and sauté for 15 minutes. When done, add juice, chicken stock and thyme, and simmer for about 20 minutes.

Cool soup, add mascarpone and purée. Serve hot or cold (I prefer it hot). Top with fried sage leaves.

Best Ever Tomato Soup

This soup has to be called "best ever" because it truly is. One fall evening, we had dinner at a restaurant in Vancouver, where I had tomato soup. It was fabulous! This my version, after a detailed conversation with our waiter.

Lots of roma tomatoes

Olive oil

Herbs of your choice (oregano, savory, garlic powder and so on)

Kosher salt

Olive oil

Fresh garlic (lots)

About 2 sweet Walla Walla onions

Celery

Fennel

Fennel pollen (available at many fresh markets)

Gin

2 L chicken stock

2 cans organic tomato paste

Lots of fresh basil

Wash the tomatoes and slice them in half. Lay them cut side up on cookie sheets that have been covered with parchment paper and drizzle with oil and herbs and a sprinkle of salt. Slow-roast the tomatoes until they shrink and seem dry. Don't let them burn. When they are done, set them aside.

Sauté the rest of the veggies in olive oil and fennel pollen. Add a splash of gin, chicken stock and tomato paste. Simmer until the flavours really meld.

Add the tomatoes and let the mixture cool, then add lots of fresh basil. Blend well.

★ **Never put hot soup in the blender to purée it. You will have the soup all over you and the kitchen—it must be very cool. Hand-held immersion blenders work very well and avoid the mess of a traditional blender.**

Turkey Soup

One day when Don and I got up to walk Misha, it was overcast and drizzling—a perfect day for turkey. With summer over and fall entering our world, we decided to find a fresh turkey. Granville Island had just sold their last fresh one a few minutes before we got there, and the same thing happened at the local meat market. At last, we found a fifteen-pound turkey at Whole Foods. So on the first day of autumn, we enjoyed fresh roasted turkey, and the next day I made soup with the leftovers. My recipe, of course, is a throw-in one—add what you like!

Cooked turkey

Butter

Onions

Garlic

Celery

Carrots and any other veggies you have on hand

Sweet potato (optional)

Corn (optional)

About 2 L chicken stock

Good-quality pasta, cooked

Leftover gravy

Fresh parsley, chopped

Poultry seasoning of your choice

Chop and sauté the onions, garlic and celery with a little butter in a heavy-bottomed pot. In a food processor, chop the carrots and any other veggies you want to add. Add these to the pot with the chicken stock and cook.

If you want to use corn, process it with a little milk and cream and add it after the other veggies are cooked. (I find the corn mush gives a very interesting sweet flavour.) Add cooked pasta if you wish.

Cut up your leftover turkey with scissors. Add as much as you like to the pot, then finish with several tablespoons of leftover gravy, chopped fresh parsley and whatever poultry seasonings you like.

Serve hot. This soup freezes well and is a great lunch treat!

My Chicken Soup

I have eaten a lot of chicken soup, and I think mine is the best!

6 skinless, boneless, free-range, good-quality chicken breasts

3 L chicken stock (or more)

8 carrots, peeled and chopped

5 parsnips, peeled and chopped

1 or 2 onions, chopped

Several leeks, well washed and chopped (white part only)

6 stalks celery, chopped

Some fresh or frozen peas

A handful of pea pods

Good-quality pasta, cooked

Lots of fresh parsley, chopped

Salt and pepper

Bake the chicken breasts, then cool and cut them up into bite-sized pieces.

Simmer all the veggies in the stock until cooked, then add the cooked chicken and pasta. If you wish, you can add a little cream or a container of creamy mushroom pasta sauce at the end. Top with parsley and salt and pepper, and serve hot.

★ **For a creamier version of this soup, purée some cream of corn soup and strain it through a sieve into your chicken soup. (I use my own cream of corn soup or a very good organic one.) When you add the yellow creamy mixture to the chicken soup, it gives the appearance of cream and gives the soup a nice, slightly sweet, mellow flavour.**

Lentil Soup

This is one of my all-time favourites, but my kids—well, they hated it. Lunchtime at our house would go something like, "Mom, please can we have ravioli from a can? It's easy—throw it in a bowl and microwave it. Or Kraft Dinner? All the kids at school get to eat that for lunch, and they get to sit in front of the TV and watch *The Flintstones*." I'd say, "No way! At my house, we eat real food and sit at the table for our meals. We have conversation and exchange ideas. Have some more lentil soup!" And on it went.

Sauté several onions and several heads of garlic in a little oil in a stock pot—just cook slightly. (The pot must have a heavy bottom—these pots may be expensive, but will last a lifetime and are really worth the investment.)

Add the lentils to the pot with the onions, garlic, chicken stock and ham bone. When the lentils are mushy (it should take about 45 minutes on low heat), add the veggies and ketchup. The cubed ham should be tossed in near the end of the cooking time.

Remove the bone and serve the soup hot or freeze for later.

Lots of garlic, finely chopped

Lots of onions, chopped

2 cups lentils, washed and checked for little stones

2 L chicken stock

Ham bone, if you have it

Carrots, chopped

Parsnips, chopped

Cabbage, chopped

Celery, chopped

Broccoli, chopped

Cauliflower, chopped

Winter squash, chopped

Spinach, chopped

Organic canned tomatoes

Canned chickpeas

Ketchup to taste

Good-quality low-sodium ham, cooked and cubed

★ **Running the veggies through the food processor before you add them to the lentils speeds up the cooking time. Sometimes I add also a little cumin to give it kick.**

Behind the Beaded Door

WE HAVE DRIVEN PAST the little shop on Pender Island with the hanging beaded door many times. Don often says we should check it out, but I am not interested. It feels too hippie for my cautious self. I am quite sure something strange lurks behind those beads.

We ask around. The locals tell us it is a grocery store owned and run by a man named John, who supports local producers and carries different things he picks up in town. "In town" means Victoria.

My curiosity overrides my caution, and one Wednesday morning we venture in through the beads for a look. I like to think of myself as a foodie and, to my utter surprise, on the other side of the beads lies a foodie heaven.

I can hardly believe my eyes. We enter a porch-like area that houses a clear glass counter, home to a lovely selection of baked goodies; steaming coffee is being served to a cluster of folks relaxing and chatting in overstuffed chairs. The surrounding walls have shelves piled high with fresh produce, mostly organic, waiting to be purchased.

Walking farther into the store, we see beautiful baskets laden with fresh artisanal bread from "town," and more shelves holding fancy oils, vinegars, biscuits and the type of canned food you usually see at high-end shops in Vancouver. The coolers are filled with meats and poultry sourced from ethical butchers.

On the tiny wooden counter lies a lined note-book with handwritten orders on it, for the next rip into town. John appears to run the store under the watchful eyes of a group of wise women of a certain age. They seem to keep him focused and organized.

John is particularly proud of the plump, luscious tomatoes he brings in, and he should be. They are as tasty as they look.

So every Tuesday and Thursday, after the 3 p.m. ferry docks on Pender—bringing John's van and a load of fine food—we visit his store to load up on great fresh produce for our evening salads.

One day, I go to pick up some tomatoes and something feels different. Maybe it is the flowers or the fresh paint, I'm not sure. I ask one of the ladies where John is. "He has retired and moved to Victoria," she replies.

A wave of sadness and loss sweeps through me. I never even knew John's last name, but for me, he was a big part of island culture. Now both John and the beaded door are gone from Pender Island.

Split Pea Soup

I love split pea soup! I remember the wonderful smells in my grandmother's kitchen when she prepared this. She served it with fresh warm biscuits and cheese. What a wonderful lunch on a cold winter day!

About 1½ lb boneless, low-fat ham, chopped

Some ham bones from your butcher

1 package split peas (the yellow variety)

2 L or more chicken stock (you may want to use up to 4, so have more handy)

An assortment of veggies, peeled and chopped (carrots, cabbage, celery, onions, parsnips, broccoli, spinach, cauliflower and so on)

In a very large soup pot with a heavy bottom, combine all ingredients except the chopped ham. Cook for several hours. Remove the bones and add the ham, then continue cooking until the peas are soft. You may wish to toss in some spices, such as marjoram or thyme, or go the curry and cumin route—either or neither would be fine.

Serve hot. This recipe makes a very large amount of soup, so be prepared to freeze some.

★ **Slow cookers are great for split pea soup. Start it in the morning and come home to a yummy, hearty soup and a great smelling home.**

Marion's Borscht

My friend Marion has been in my life forever and then some. We have lived in different cities, done different things, but we always find our way back to each other. It is Marion who I get into artistic trouble and fun with, for she too is creative. Today we are both writers. Not long ago, while on a winter retreat on Pender Island, Marion said to me, "Noni, get that cookbook finished and off your desk!"

1 lb spareribs (the small ones)

6 cups water

6 beets, shredded

1 onion, chopped

1 carrot, shredded

1 potato, shredded

1 can tomato paste

2 L chicken stock

Simmer the ribs in the water for 1 hour. When cooked and cool enough to handle, remove the meat from the bones, skim the fat from the water and add the veggies to the rib water. Cook for 45 minutes, then add the tomato paste and as much stock as you wish. Continue cooking for another 30 minutes.

Serve chunky and hot.

You and I Have Shared So Much

I'M REFLECTING ON A long and special friendship. Fortunately, our parents chose to live in the same neighbourhood, setting the stage for a lifelong relationship.

We supported our parents as they aged, became ill and passed. We eventually returned to the family neighbourhood, where we now own homes. Coincidentally, for a time in our lives we both called South Granville home.

We have watched our children grow through adventures and misadventures. Sometimes I felt as if I were growing up with your children. As time passed, all of our children developed into fine adults. I love hearing news of your children and grandchildren. I believe your greatest work of art is your family.

Our husbands love us, work hard and provide well.

We have shared ideas and materials, always supporting each other. Later, we began to write together. You kindly invited me to join your writing group. Writing was something I had never done before, but I love it. Now we meet every year for a writers' retreat.

We have laughed our way through making Christmas decorations and selling almost none. Those times of shared activities have been some of the happiest of my life. With you by my side, anything is possible. At this period in our lives it is more difficult to accomplish that close working relationship, but we do a pretty good job over the phone and through visits.

We have had endless lunches at the Upper Crust Café and wonderful dinners at your home and ours. We have also enjoyed good local spots for an evening out. We have worked together and separately on beautiful table settings and centrepieces. We have collected rocks and special papers, and picked saskatoonberries together. We have walked and biked and shared recipes. You have taught me almost all I know about flowers and gardening.

We have been partners in crime, liberating two rosebush cuttings from the university. We rationalized it, saying we could provide a better home for the cuttings, and they would probably destroy the bushes anyway to build yet another building—and they did. Your rosebush grew into a huge rose tree. Mine died. Last year you kindly brought a cutting from your bush to Pender Island. Sadly, it died too.

We have discussed our projects together as we explored all forms of art. We also worked on decorating and creating beautiful homes. None is more perfect than yours.

And, of course, we both love a wee glass of good red wine!

And so, my friend, our lives are like one of our weavings: one of us is the weft and the other the warp. Alternating positions depending on the situation, each in a caring, supportive role.

You have done so many wonderful things on your life journey and continue to embark on new and exciting adventures, always embracing life fully with joy and enthusiasm.

The other day I got off the phone with you and said to Don, "I am so very lucky to have Marion in my life. She lights up my life and shares her true goodness."

My one wish for myself would be to be more like you. I love Vancouver, but I really miss you.

Sandwiches, Pizzas and Lunches

Rolled Asparagus Sandwiches

TWO WAYS

Some people like to toast the first way or fry the rolls in butter in a nonstick frying pan. Use a soft, good-quality sandwich bread, with the crust cut off. Serve them warm or chilled, as you like.

FIRST WAY

Good-quality sandwich bread, crust removed

Herbed cream or goat cheese

Asparagus spears

Thinly spread each slice of bread with herbed cream or goat cheese. Place 2 or 3 asparagus spears diagonally on the slices and roll.

SECOND WAY

Good-quality sandwich bread, crust removed

Egg salad, mashed

Asparagus spears

Thinly spread finely mashed egg salad on the bread slices. Place the asparagus spears on top and roll.

Tuna Melts

Who doesn't love a tuna melt on a chilly day? We certainly do.

Canned tuna

Green onions, chopped

Green olives (with pimento), chopped

Red pepper, finely chopped

Sweet pickle, chopped

Mayonnaise

Good bread

Good cheddar

Make a tuna salad using the green onions, olives, red pepper and sweet pickle. Mix with mayonnaise. Place the tuna salad on toast or bread and top with cheddar. Melt under the broiler and serve with a light green salad.

★ **The olives are a must.**

Salmon Salad Sandwiches

This is one of my long-time favourites. Use a good, chewy, whole-grain bread.

★ **Use fresh lemon instead of bottled lemon juice. Fresh lemons can be stored whole in a resealable plastic bag in the fridge. Bigger, rounder lemons tend to be more juicy.**

Fresh poached salmon
(or canned skinless and boneless sockeye)

Miracle Whip

Green onion, finely chopped

Splash of fresh lemon juice

Lettuce, shredded

Cucumber, sliced

Fresh dill

Good bread

Mix the salmon with Miracle Whip, green onion and lemon juice. Top with lettuce, cucumber and fresh dill and serve on your favourite bread.

Under the Arbutus Tree

NINE FRIENDS, WHO ALL come from different backgrounds, are gathering for lunch under the shade of an ancient arbutus tree one warm summer day on Bowen Island.

We meet in the morning in busy downtown Vancouver, a wonderful city that seems to draw people to its gentle shores. We board an express bus to Horseshoe Bay, and then a ferry takes us on the short trip to Bowen Island, where we have a lunch reservation.

As we sip white wine, a soft ocean breeze floats past us, while the sun warms our bare arms.

I am pleased to be part of such an interesting group of friends.

Celine, our only French Canadian member, talks with her hands flying expressively in every direction. I love her incredible energy. Across from her, Amira, a bank executive, talks about her volunteer work with young girls in her Muslim community.

Alexa, a successful entrepreneur, shares her ups and downs of opening a new high-end boutique. A single mom, she has worked for thirty years to get to this place, and she has made it! The opening was more wonderful than she had hoped for.

Jen, our organizer extraordinaire, a professional accountant and international tax expert, directs us to focus on our menus as our server visits the table for the second time. "Focus, girls, focus." We order, and quickly return to visiting.

Barbara, an accomplished author, tells us about a new book she is working on and how she visits schools to help kids read.

Across the table, Dani listens quietly. Her story is probably one of the bravest I have heard. Years ago, Dani and her then husband left their baby boy with her mother in Bulgaria, which was under Communist rule at the time, to fly on a holiday to Cuba. When the plane stopped in on Newfoundland to refuel, they left all their belongings behind, got off the plane and applied for refugee status. Dani, a professional nurse, worked any job she could get and sometimes several at the same time. Eventually she was able to get her son to Canada and establish a stable, professional life. But not without a lot of heartache and courage.

Lucy is the most colourful of our diverse group of women. I don't know her very well, having met her only a few times. She is a traveller, and I think her life has been really difficult. Today, she is single and seeing all of North America in a small Boler trailer. She pulls it behind a large 4-by-4 truck. I ask, "Aren't you scared, all by yourself in these remote places so far from home?" I am fascinated with her tales. "No," she answers. "I feel totally safe." Apparently, she overnights in Walmart parking lots, placing a pair of size 12 men's work boots outside the trailer door. Wow, this lady has it all worked out. I really admire her independent spirit.

Lunch comes and we all enjoy not only the food, but also our unique surroundings. These coastal islands are so different from the mainland. Life here is more casual and definitely slower.

Over coffee, Pat tells us all tales of growing up on a farm in Saskatchewan. I listen, gobsmacked. They had no indoor plumbing. Can you imagine using an outhouse in minus-twenty-degree weather with gale winds blowing blinding snow in every direction? She tells stories of going to a small school in a wagon. In spring, stones rise to the surface and must be removed before the farm fields can be planted. This was done with something called a "stone boat," a large flat wooden sleigh that horses dragged along while the family picked up the stones and packed them on board. Today Pat is a really gifted artist, showing her work in fine galleries.

Lunch done, "the girls" decide to explore the shops. I choose to sit and gaze out over the blue ocean to the mountains above Howe Sound—the view is breathtaking. I am so fortunate to be in this majestic West Coast location with such amazing women, who would never let you know just how accomplished they all are.

My mind wanders and I reflect on the diversity of friends we are free to have in Canada. For me Canada feels akin to a large pie, with every slice a gift from a different culture and place.

Open-Faced Sandwiches

Here are some of my favourite combinations. I like to use really good bread. Brush it with olive oil or, if appropriate, an oil infused with garlic. Toasting the bread is optional.

Caprese Roast fresh roma tomatoes with lots of garlic and oregano. When the tomatoes are done, spread them on the toast or bread and top with sliced buffalo-milk cheese and lots of fresh basil.

Cheese and Fig Spread a generous amount of cambozola cheese (or cheese of your choice) on the toast or bread. Broil in the oven until it melts, and top with fresh fig slices and arugula. Make sure to use fresh figs.

Egg Spread egg salad mixture on the toast or bread. Top with real bacon bits. Next, add fresh asparagus (just barely cooked, you want it crisp and tender). Top with lots of spinach. Drizzle a small amount of oil and vinegar dressing on the spinach.

Ham and Cheese Spread herbed Philadelphia cream cheese on a slice of bread and top with good ham and a good pickle.

Shrimp Spread basil pesto on toast or bread. Place poached shrimp, cut in half lengthwise, on the pesto. Top with thinly sliced avocado and a sprinkle of feta cheese.

Turkey Spread cranberry chutney on the toast or bread. Top with thinly sliced turkey. Spread a thin layer of garlic aioli on the turkey, then top with a pile of mixed baby greens.

Veggie Spread a thick layer of hummus on the toast or bread. Add a layer of thinly sliced radishes, then a layer of thinly sliced cucumber. Sprinkle with toasted pine nuts and chopped Italian parsley. Top with a pile of young greens.

Pizza Dough

We have an Italian pizza oven on Pender Island, so we often all gather in our large country kitchen, where we participate in pizza making. I am still trying to perfect my dough—I have not achieved exactly what I want yet. To date I have had perfect dough in two places: Una Pizza in Calgary and a new place on West Fourth Avenue in Vancouver. Both have a wonderful end product ... a thin, flavourful crust, not soggy or soft.

★ I usually partially bake the dough, then either freeze it for later use or top it (see page 95) and finish baking it as a pizza.

1 tbsp dry instant yeast

½ cup warm water

1 tsp sugar

2 to 3 cups flour (I use pizza flour)

½ tsp salt

⅓ cup olive oil

½ cup sparkling water or beer

Dissolve the yeast in warm water and sugar. Mix with the rest of the ingredients for about 4 minutes using a dough hook. Place the dough in a resealable bag in the fridge for 24 hours.

The next day, divide the dough into portions and gently flatten and stretch into circles. Don't overwork the dough. Set the dough aside to rest and rise until ready to bake.

Pizza Toppings

Here are a few great options to top your homemade pizza dough. When using a regular oven, I cook my pizzas at about 425 degrees—but always keep an eye on them and use your own judgement. I like to use a round, flat mesh pan to cook them on—I found mine at The Gourmet Warehouse in Vancouver.

★ Pizza can be great for a tapas party, too. Just make a tiny, hand-held version of the same thing! The trick is to keep them small and easy to manage—don't add too many toppings. Basil, arugula and truffle oil is a good combination to try.

Danish Danish fontina cheese and fresh mozzarella cheese, sautéed and well-drained mushrooms (they need to be dry) and wild arugula. Drizzle with truffle oil.

Greek Cooked ground lamb sausage and goat cheese. Top with fresh mint and roasted garlic.

Hoisin My daughter Suzanne shared this with me and we love it! Use hoisin sauce; diced chicken sautéed in salt, pepper and soy sauce; green onion, bean sprouts and lots of mozzarella.

Kid's Just tomato sauce with some cheese and salami. I once made eighty of these for a party in Calgary.

Pear and Walnut Basil pesto, toasted walnuts, thinly sliced pears, red onions (thinly sliced and slowly cooked in a good balsamic vinegar) and your choice (or a mix) of mozzarella, burrata or Danish fontina. Top with arugula after cooking.

Pender Fig Figs, walnuts, Salt Spring Island cheese and prosciutto. Add grated fontina prior to heating.

Quick Lunch Use naan instead of pizza dough. Brush with a bit of olive oil and mashed roasted garlic, and roast in the oven to crisp. Top lightly with a tomato sauce, steamed asparagus, red peppers, sliced mushrooms or any veggies you have around. Place some buffalo mozzarella on top and broil for a few minutes.

Roasted Cremini Mushroom and Truffle Oil Roast some cremini mushrooms and top with mozzarella. Once heated, top with fresh arugula, truffle oil and grated Parmesan.

Roasted Pender Tomato Cheese, basil and roasted tomatoes. Add fresh basil after heating.

Sweet Chili Chicken Another delightful pizza from Suzanne. Use a half-and-half mix of tomato sauce and sweet chili sauce. Top with diced chicken (sautéed in sweet chili sauce, salt and pepper), pineapple, green onion and lots of mozzarella.

Loss of a Lunch Friend

TIME—THERE IS NEVER ENOUGH. We leave for the airport shortly, heading to Vancouver. Keeping an eye on the clock, I struggle with my pantyhose, one leg in, one out. I deeply dislike wearing them. It's the droopy crotch ones I loathe the most. Nothing makes me crabbier. The problem is that they all look so innocent in the drawer; it isn't until you wear them for a while that you know if you have saggy, baggy droopers or okay hose. (Later I discover Wolford pantyhose, which stay up and work really well.)

"Oh well, here's hoping!" I mutter as I pull the other leg partly in. Sharp rings from the phone interrupt my task. I stumble and hop across the room. A voice comes from the front hall: "You don't have time for that now," my husband calls.

"Right. I'll get the message as we leave," I say.

While waiting for the cab I have time to quickly access the message. The words are crisp and clear. My friend Mary's voice fills our front hall. "I don't want to be your friend any longer. I will return your books and tapes. Goodbye." Shock surges through me. I feel stunned and stung. I have just been dumped. As I digest the blow, our cab arrives and off we go. Later, on the plane, I will have time to think.

Our plane takes off, reflection takes over and reality sets in. I have been released from a friendship. Did I deserve the dumping? Sitting in solitude, I allow myself to feel. Slowly, ever so slowly, dismay and distress pass and I begin to feel relief. Is it possible this ending is something both Mary and I wanted and needed? That only she had the courage to act?

I wonder if a dying friendship is akin to a terminal illness. Bumping along, sometimes painful, sometimes in remission, finally taking the last few gasps, and then expiring. In the end it was a small thing that dealt the final blow. Mary wanted me to be available for an event and I chose not to be. Sadly, I feel the moment speaks of our different lives now. Both of us wanted growth and change. It came, with each of us choosing very separate paths.

My eyes drift out the aircraft window. Crossing the Rockies never fails to fill me with wonder. Today we have a clear blue sky. The sun is dancing playfully over and around the snowy mountains, dipping into valleys below and settling on the frozen lakes and streams. Rigid trees appear covered in frost. A magical peace blankets our amazing vista.

Mary and I met in winter. We were both newly single and in our early forties. In those days we seemed to have so much in common: work, clothes, books, lunches, and men and dating. We spent endless hours sipping lattes, questioning and exploring the mysteries of the human male, dating now as compared to when we were young.

And, of course, work. Even in those apparently perfect times our dissimilarities began surfacing. In an attempt to keep all well, I suppose we both covered up things that we felt uncomfortable with. Many fundamental differences appeared as we became comfortable and our authentic selves emerged.

As single, mid-aged people, our idea of fun and recreation began to diverge. I am a morning person, happily in bed early with a book. I put great value on my friendships built when I had been first married, maintaining connections with those couples wherever possible. Mary chose to release the folks from her past. My friend was far more glamorous than I, choosing exciting clothing, dancing and dating the nights away. She plays in a band, sings and has a great time. I don't like bars and my dancing skills are almost non-existent, plus all those activities begin in the evening as I am picking up a good book. While I become more sedate, her activity becomes more colourful. Then I met and married my husband, increasing our contrasting life choices even more. What remained was our joy in lunching together.

As the flight lands at Vancouver International Airport, I accept that we, Mary and I, are diverse. Not good or bad, just the way it is.

I am conscious of a stray tear, quickly blotting it. The flight attendant is announcing our final descent.

Once safely landed, my husband goes to the luggage carousel and I go to the washroom, where I remove my pantyhose. They are droopers. As I pass the trash, I toss them in, telling myself it is time to be mindful, paying attention when things no longer fit and taking good care to nurture those things that do. We gather our luggage and head out into the Vancouver dampness. Large drops of rain splash on my face and bare legs. I feel free to explore new beginnings and savour old friendships.

Steak Sandwiches

These are good served with a side of greens, such as arugula with red beet tops, radishes and cucumber.

Steak, medium-rare and thinly sliced

Focaccia, toasted

Garlic, crushed

Butter

Mayonnaise

Onions, caramelized with thyme

Mix the garlic with butter and spread onto the toasted bread. Top first with mayo, then with the cooked steak and onion mixture.

My Mom's Party Ham Sandwiches

These sandwiches appeared at countless lunches, showers and teas, and also on Bridge night. It's one of my all-time favourite recipes—even back in Grade 6, I used to take a shoebox full of these, crust removed, to share with friends (along with a jar of chocolate milk and a few choco-mallow cookies).

Ham

Celery, minced

Hardboiled eggs

Green relish

Hot-dog mustard

Green onions, chopped

Mayonnaise

Pepper

White bread, crust removed

In a food processor, lightly chop a good-quality piece of ham. Don't over-process. Place in a bowl and mix with all of the remaining ingredients. Serve on fresh white bread with the crust removed.

★ **To make an old-fashioned version, use baloney instead of ham, yellow onion instead of green and sweet pickles instead of relish.**

Quiche

When I make a quiche, I like to punch holes in the bottom of a foil pan to help with the baking process. If the quiche is for entertaining, I do it in an Emile Henry pie pan, in which I pre-bake the pastry slightly before adding my ingredients.

Pastry (see page 264)

Grated cheese of your choice

Spinach or asparagus, chopped

Cooked bacon bits or chopped ham

4 to 6 eggs, plus some additional egg white

About ¾ cup milk or cream

Dust the bottom of the pastry with some flour. Add the cheese and vegetables, then cover with bacon or ham. Mix the eggs and cream and pour overtop.

Bake at 350 degrees, lowering to 325 or 300 if it is baking too quickly. Be prepared: it often takes longer than you'd expect.

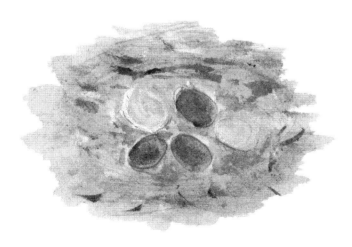

Salads

Watermelon Salad

This goes great with lamb kebobs!

Watermelon, cubed

Red onion, sliced

Feta cheese

Mint leaves, torn

Kalamata olives

Butter lettuce

Toss with your favourite oil and vinegar dressing and serve.

Our Caesar Salad

The key ingredients in this dressing's success are the lemon and the garlic.

One head of crisp romaine lettuce

Coarsely grated Parmesan cheese (use a potato peeler)

Garlic croutons (homemade is best)

Raw cauliflower, cut into pieces (optional)

DRESSING

½ cup Kraft Creamy Caesar dressing

3 or 4 cloves fresh garlic, chopped finely

Dollop of good olive oil

Fresh lemon juice

Thyme

1 tbsp Worcestershire sauce

Anchovies, finely chopped (optional)

Toss together the salad ingredients. Mix the dressing and pour over the salad.

Garden Tomato Salad

I like using garden-fresh heritage tomatoes for this salad.

Tomatoes

Farmhouse cheese, in chunks

Balsamic vinegar dressing

Bread crumbs or panko

Fresh basil

Cut tomatoes into chunks. Mix with cheese and a basic balsamic dressing. Add spicy bread crumbs (panko is good) and top with a variety of fresh basil.

Kale Salad

This is like a kale Caesar, similar to one served at popular restaurant in Calgary.

Kale, chopped

Bacon bits (homemade is best)

Hardboiled egg

Grated Parmesan

Any good Caesar dressing

Toasted panko crumbs (I like the seasoned President's Choice brand)

Toss the kale, bacon bits, hardboiled egg and cheese in with your favourite Caesar dressing (you can use just the whites of the egg if you want a lighter salad). Top with the panko crumbs and serve.

We Do Not Steal

APPARENTLY I AM A THIEF at five years of age, having just liberated a good-sized handful of sticky gold stars from their tiny box, located on a shelf just the right height for a bored child. My mother and grandmother are busy finishing their transaction. Our location is the High Level pharmacy in Edmonton.

Walking home, I proudly open my now-sticky hand to show my new treasure. As the shiny stars glitter in the sun, my mother gasps. "Noni, that is stealing. We must take them right back." Unceremoniously, I am marched back to the pharmacy, where I return my booty and, worse, am forced to acknowledge what I have done and apologize to the proprietor.

Years pass and the pharmacy morphs into one new business after another. Finally, the spot where I first engaged in criminal activity becomes a bistro named the Highlevel Diner. The ancient, rickety building overlooks the North Saskatchewan River and is a short walk from the University of Alberta. It is very appealing to the granola/hippie crowd, including me.

In this warm, eclectic bistro with mismatched chairs and old wooden tables, a good part of my life unfolds. Here, I journey through happy and sad times—both my own and those of my friends and family—as I am now a regular.

Major events in my life occur in this diner: my first date with Don, my last lunch with my dad before he dies. Endless coffees, brunches, lunches and dinners with friends happen here. One Valentine's Day, Don asks me to marry him, and gives me a lovely diamond ring. All of these moments and many more occur at one or another of its bistro tables.

The small group of young folk that own the diner strive to prepare fresh, local home-cooked food. The popular bistro makes amazing cinnamon buns in the morning, and for lunch and supper serves not-to-be-missed burgers, plus home cut fries and the best in-house ketchup (see page 259 to make it yourself).

The bun recipe is quite famous and can be found on the internet by searching "U of A famous tuck shop buns."

Even today, on a frigid winter morning, you will see a long line from the front door around the block, all waiting to be welcomed in and seated at one of the cozy tables. For me, it's a place where a pile of memories exists between the walls.

Spinach Salad

TWO WAYS

FIRST WAY

Spinach

Thinly sliced sweet onions

Bacon bits (homemade is best)

Fresh sliced mushrooms

Dried cranberries

Toasted almonds

Hardboiled egg, diced (optional)

DRESSING

1 large dollop of low-fat Miracle Whip

A dollop of buttermilk

Fresh lemon juice

A dollop of canola oil

Hy's Seasoning Salt

Pepper

Thyme

Fresh garlic, mashed

Mix salad, mix dressing, toss and serve!

SECOND WAY

Spinach

A handful of toasted almonds

1 small head of cauliflower, broken into florets

DRESSING

½ cup grapeseed oil

2 tbsp soy sauce

2 tbsp malt vinegar

Small amount of grated ginger

Pinch of salt

1 tbsp brown sugar

Combine and serve, just like the first way.

I love a good, fresh spinach salad— for a while, I made one of these every Saturday when I came home from the market. Be sure to only use fresh, clean spinach.

Sweet Slaw My Way

I use an Asian dressing for this salad.

★ **Try growing your own herbs—chives, mint, rosemary and parsley are all very hardy. When growing mint make sure to contain it, because it loves to spread.**

Savoy cabbage, finely chopped

Red cabbage, finely chopped

Fresh mint, chopped

Italian parsley, chopped

Red peppers, sliced

Mango, sliced

Papaya, sliced

Red chili flakes

Sweet onion, finely chopped

Your choice of salad dressing

Nuts, such as peanuts,
almonds or macadamias, toasted

Toss salad with a dressing, then top with toasted nuts of your choice.

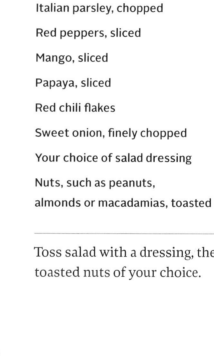

Bean Salad

Adjust the ingredient quantities in this salad to suit your tastes. Feel free to add other veggies or omit ones you don't like.

Mix salad ingredients and dress. Keep in the refrigerator until ready to serve.

1 can chickpeas, drained and rinsed

1 can red kidney beans, drained and rinsed

1 can black beans, drained and rinsed

1 small package of frozen corn, cooked and cooled

1 cup celery, chopped

1 sweet onion, chopped

1 red pepper, chopped

1 small zucchini, chopped

DRESSING

½ cup red wine vinegar

½ cup fresh basil, chopped

⅓ cup good-quality olive oil

1 tbsp Dijon mustard

1 clove garlic, minced

½ tsp hot sauce

Salt and pepper

My Bulgur Salad

I like to serve this salad with cold poached salmon.

1 cup bulgur

About a dozen cherry tomatoes, cut in half (or 6 to 8 medium, chopped)

1 bunch steamed asparagus, chopped and chilled

1 bunch green onions, chopped

1 cup chickpeas, rinsed and drained

1 cup chopped parsley

1 small jar artichoke hearts, drained, rinsed and sliced

1 cup of pitted black olives (optional)

Fresh salad greens

DRESSING

Olive oil

Fresh lemon juice

Salt and pepper

TOPPING

Feta cheese

Lemon slices

In a pot, bring 1½ cups of water to a boil; add the bulgur. Cover and remove from the heat, then let sit for 20 minutes. Drain and cool.

Once the bulgur is cool, combine all of the salad ingredients except the greens. Toss with the dressing, then place the dressed salad on top of the greens. Top with crumbled feta and serve with fresh lemon slices on the side.

★ **Use your nose when picking asparagus. If there is a bad smell, keep walking. To store, cut the ends off and store upright in just enough cold water to cover the base.**

Broccoli Salad

One of the best broccoli salads I have ever had was at my sister-in-law Shelagh's place. She is a master gardener and knows how to make good use of her produce. This is a version of her salad.

★ **Stabilize a basic vinaigrette by adding a half teaspoon of mayonnaise.**

About 3 large broccoli stalks, washed and chopped

One sweet onion, sliced

One red pepper, chopped

A handful of dried cranberries

A handful of toasted almonds

Some crushed dried basil and oregano

Your choice of salad dressing

Mix and dress with a good oil and lemon/vinegar dressing, or use a commercial Italian dressing.

String Bean and Broccoli Salad

This recipe takes about three pounds of a combination of beans and broccoli. It can be doubled for a crowd.

String beans, trimmed

Broccoli, chopped

DRESSING

¼ cup olive oil

1 tsp toasted sesame oil

1 tsp light soy sauce

1 tbsp red wine vinegar

Salt and pepper

1 tbsp peanut butter

TOPPING

Sesame seeds, toasted

Green onion, finely chopped

Red pepper, sliced into thin strips

Blanch the beans and broccoli. Mix the dressing ingredients together and fold into the vegetables. Top with sesame, green onion and red pepper. Serve cold or hot.

★ **Slivered almonds make a great alternate topping for this.**

The Famous Stainless Steel Salad Bowl to the Rescue

I **AM A CITY PERSON**—always have been. Until this point in my life, travel has been by plane or train. I am not acquainted with rural Canada. I suppose I have always viewed the country as an in-between place… until the famous May long weekend.

I am in a relationship with a man named Don, who later becomes my husband. He loves adventure and challenge; with me, he is about to experience both—and vice versa.

The plan is a camping trip. It begins with a small glitch… me. Aside from the fact that I am totally unfamiliar with camping, I am unwell. I have just had minor surgery that turned out to be not so minor. Not serious, but very painful indeed. If you have ever had bottom end surgery, such as an episiotomy or hemorrhoid repair, you will understand my troubles. I have trouble both sitting and walking. Also, I have just done a naughty thing. To get out of the hospital, I lied to the nurses, telling them I had passed water (peed) when I had not. There is no way I am going to let them catheterize me and keep me in the hospital overnight. I want to be free. Anyway, I can take care of myself, I reason. Besides, I am curious about this camping thing and we really aren't that far from the city.

So, I start this recovery on the wrong foot. With only two days before the trip I'm really not doing very well. I can't pass water easily even in my own home. I am in intense pain, allergic to the pain medication and vomiting. Maybe my choices were unwise. Don kindly steps in and takes over both my care and planning the expedition with great gusto—neither of us even considers cancelling the trip.

My daughters and friends urge me to reconsider. "Go later," they say. "Go the July long weekend." No way; I want to be a good sport, open to new adventures and experiences. "Maybe a couple of days away would be a good thing," I tell them. "It was just minor surgery after all."

Friday afternoon is upon us and I am not a lot better, but I choose to keep this information to myself. Don's tiny Boler trailer is attached to his red Jeep and ready to go. I am a little uneasy as I carefully walk out to the vehicle with my new best friend—a rubber doughnut—under my arm.

I push my fears down and tell myself that I can and will do this trip.

Camping with Don is a procedure, quite unlike how I would do it—I go into everything with a list and a plan, but my future husband likes to follow his heart, packing by going up and down the aisles at Superstore and throwing everything that seems useful in the cart. I am too weak to participate in the decision-making or protest his methods, so I just follow along, using the cart to hold myself upright.

We have an idea about what a sitz bath would do for me—it could be comfortable and healing. Off to housewares we go to look for a vessel to hold warm water. We scan the aisles and decide a salad bowl might work. However, sizing might be a bit of a problem. How does one try sitting in a salad bowl in Superstore? Well, you do it carefully! Wait until the aisle is clear, then bend over and stick your butt in the bowl while your accomplice pushes it into place to get a good fit. We toss the stainless steel salad bowl into our cart and head to the checkout with our treasures.

I shuffle to the Jeep, exhausted, sink into my old friend the rubber doughnut, and off we go. Dusk falls, followed by darkness, as we motor along back roads to a place in the middle of nowhere, deep in the forest.

As we arrive at our weekend destination, Don carefully parks the Jeep and trailer parallel to a small, rocky stream. Tall trees surround our camping spot. We are absolutely alone. The only sound is the babbling brook. Darkness envelops us; the only light comes from clusters of twinkling stars above. "Where did all those stars come from?" I ask. Don explains, "They are always out there but you can't see them as well in the city."

Don sets up camp. Wood is collected, a fire started. We place two chairs in front of the fire. The setting is truly magical. But alas, all is not well. I am much, much worse. I collapse onto my rubber ring and bend my head into my arms and weep. I feel like I want to die. I am in pain, and the nearest hospital—and catheter—is sixty kilometres away.

Never fear; Don is resourceful! He warms water and pours it into the stainless steel salad bowl. I pop a pill and he hands me a glass of champagne followed by my favourite— a hot dog on a willow stick. I am now sitting in my sitz bath, champagne in one hand, roasting a wiener with the other. Recovery begins in the middle of nowhere, Alberta!

AN EPILOGUE

"WHAT BECAME OF the stainless steel salad bowl?" you ask. I hesitate to answer… for a while, it stays in the trailer (I'm not sure why), and that leads to something kind of gross. A year after that first-ever camping trip, we are on a sailing weekend with acquaintances. One participant—an "about town guy"—needed a salad bowl to use for his wonderful Caesar salad. He spots our stainless steel bowl and wants it; while it's clean, of course, I hesitate and suggest he use a different one. But he insists, grabs the famous stainless steel bowl and uses it for his salad—yuck!

Guilt creeps over me… at first. But then I remember the book *The Lovely Bones* by Alice Sebold. There's a scene in it where an icicle falls on the perp's head, killing him—a sort of cosmic justice. As our acquaintance serves the salad to one of his many mistresses, I think of his partner at home and feel maybe this too is cosmic justice. My feelings of guilt evaporate.

After that trip, I get rid of the stainless steel bowl.

Carrot Salad

When I was a student nurse, the hospital often served a carrot raisin salad that I disliked intensely. The recipe below is a great improvement and is easy to make.

★ **Add chopped fresh mint as a nice alternative.**

Fresh organic carrots, peeled and grated

3 green onions, chopped

⅔ cup peanuts, coarsely chopped

DRESSING

¼ cup red wine vinegar

¼ cup canola or peanut oil

1 tsp sesame oil

1 drop hot sauce

Toss together, dress and serve.

Carrots by Donna

One Christmas about twenty years ago, our friend Donna served these with tourtière (see page 164). Since then, I have served them at many dinners, including a large gathering we had for friends who were moving.

★ **Parboil the carrots if you like them slightly softer.**

2 lb carrots, cut into coins

1 red pepper, sliced

1 green pepper, sliced

1 large sweet onion, sliced

MARINADE

1 cup tomato soup

1 tbsp dry mustard

½ cup oil

½ cup sugar

½ tsp pepper

Heat the marinade to dissolve the sugar. Pour over the chopped veggies and refrigerate for about 24 hours. Drain and serve.

Greek Salad

There are many Greek salads out there, but I think my friend Maggie makes the best one. This is her recipe.

1 head of romaine lettuce, torn

2 tomatoes, chopped

1 English cucumber, chopped

A small container of pitted kalamata olives

1 green pepper, chopped

1 red onion, chopped

½ cup celery, chopped

DRESSING

½ cup olive oil

3 tbsp lemon juice

2 tsp oregano

Salt and pepper

TOPPING

About ½ cup crumbled feta

Combine all of the salad ingredients. Toss with the dressing and top with feta.

Light Beet Salad

We once tried a salad similar to this one at the Royal Hawaiian hotel. After dinner, I wandered into the kitchen and asked how they had cut the beets, which looked like fine noodles. They said a Japanese turning slicer created the noodle look. The device is available at some kitchen specialty stores, like Williams-Sonoma or The Gourmet Warehouse, or at Japanese specialty shops.

★ **This device can create a lovely topping for a plain salad as well.**

Several cups of mixed greens

Sweet onion, sliced

White balsamic vinegar

Olive oil

Sea salt

Beets, raw and cut with a Japanese turning slicer

Toss the greens and onion with vinegar and oil to taste, then top with a bit of sea salt. Top with the raw "noodled" beets.

Rainbow Salad

I love this salad. Just start with the core ingredients and go in any direction you wish.

Combine all ingredients and toss. To give it a lift I add a splash of Boccalino Swiss European–style dressing. It's made in Canmore, Alberta, and it's also available in the produce aisle at Safeway or Save-On-Foods.

★ **If you want to save time, any commercial dressing could also do the trick.**

Fresh orange slices or segments

Yellow beets, raw and peeled, cut into matchsticks

Red beets, raw and peeled, cut into matchsticks

Carrots, raw and peeled, cut into matchsticks

Large handful English mint, chopped

Large handful Italian parsley, chopped

Red seedless organic grapes, cut in half

Toasted almond pieces

DRESSING

About 3 tbsp mixed orange and lemon juice

2 cloves garlic, mashed

A good spoonful of sugar

White wine vinegar

Splash of hot sauce

A spoonful of Dijon mustard

Olive oil

Salt and pepper

Forage Tomato and Grilled Corn Salad

Forage is a take-out shop in Calgary's Marda Loop that focuses on mostly local ingredients from sustainable farms. This salad was so delightful, and it made me feel grateful to have access to such wonderful local suppliers during the COVID pandemic. Thank you to Tagen at Forage for letting me share this recipe.

Heirloom tomatoes

Grilled fresh corn

Red onions

Parsley

Fresh thyme

Balsamic vinegar

Olive oil

Salt and pepper

Sugar

Slice the vegetables and toss with the herbs and a little bit of balsamic, olive oil, salt, pepper and sugar.

A New Way

IT IS MID-MARCH 2020, and we are packing for our winter holiday when we receive a call from Don's brother. "Have you heard the news?" he asks.

"No," I answer.

"Everything is closed," he says.

COVID-19 is here.

Don and I quickly decide to unpack our summer clothes and repack with winter and spring clothes as we are now going to Calgary, where we have a condo near our children. We plan to stay there. Wow, isolation! What will that look like? How will we cope? No close contact with anyone, no shopping for anything...

Well, to our delight and surprise, it turns out to be quite wonderful. We lose so much, but we also discover a lot of new experiences. For the first time, we are able to really clean, and make our Calgary condo feel comfortable. We paint and repair furniture, clean cupboards and create a new sitting room out of a cluttered back bedroom. I even try to learn to knit, but down deep I don't have the patience, so we'll see how that goes.

All of this, plus our groceries and food appear through something called "curbside pickup." It works really well, and we feel very fortunate to get to know three amazing locally owned businesses.

First, we find Sunnyside Natural Market, where every week we email a list of groceries, then pick up our order the next day. The orders are always filled perfectly and placed carefully in our trunk by a friendly and helpful young employee. I am so pleased with the quality of the organic produce there, and of the grass-fed whole milk.

When I need any hard-to-find ingredients or a new cookbook, I just have to phone The Cookbook Co. Cooks. Not only are they likely to have whatever it is I want, in the rare times that they don't have it, they will try to get it for me. Then we just drive up and it is placed in our trunk.

Our third wonderful find becomes a weekly treat—Forage. This little deli posts a new menu to choose from every day, with everything cooked and ready to go for curbside pickup.

One Friday night, on our way to a social distanced visit with our children, we pick up our order and it is a feast to behold. The menu includes fresh whole lobster with almost a litre of warm drawn butter, potato salad, chilled roasted asparagus, a baguette, a Romanesco salad and another salad made of tomatoes and grilled corn.

We all love the whole meal, but I am particularly amazed by the tomato and corn salad. It is an unexpected combination that I never would have thought of, but it is so flavourful and fresh! As I often do when I come across a dish that impresses me, I ask for the recipe, and they give it to me.

Potato Salad

THREE WAYS

I make three different versions of potato salad: the first is my mother's, the second is my daughter Suzanne's and the last is mine—it is a "take off" of the wonderful potato salad served at a lovely restaurant in Edmonton called the Upper Crust Café, and it is my current favourite.

★ **I never measure when making potato salad—just use your judgement.**

FIRST WAY

About 6 or 7 large white potatoes, peeled, boiled and chopped

About 4 eggs, boiled, peeled and chopped

1 bunch green onions, chopped

1 large cucumber, peeled and chopped

About 1 cup celery, chopped

Green olives stuffed with red pimento

DRESSING

Mayonnaise or Miracle Whip

Buttermilk

A few squirts of hot-dog mustard

A few spoons of sweet relish

Fresh dill, chopped

Salt and pepper

Add the dressing ingredients to the veggies and toss.

SECOND WAY

8 to 10 red potatoes, boiled and chopped

About ¼ cup of pickle liquid

Sour cream

Mayonnaise

About ½ tsp creamy horseradish (optional)

Green onions, chopped

Fresh dill, chopped

Salt and pepper

When the potatoes are cooked and drained, place them in a bowl and cover with some liquid from a jar of dill pickles. While the potatoes are still hot, add sour cream and mayonnaise to cover. Add horseradish if you wish, then add some chopped green onion, dill, salt and pepper. Chill and serve.

THIRD WAY

Mix of red and white potatoes

½ cup white vinegar

⅛ cup grapeseed oil

Fresh dill, chopped

Green onions, chopped

Mayonnaise

Boil the potatoes—do not peel. When cooked, drain well and place in a glass bowl.

Pour vinegar and grapeseed oil over the hot potatoes. Let them cool, then add lots of chopped fresh dill and green onions. Mix in mayonnaise to taste and chill.

Mixed Squash Salad

This recipe is just a list—add whatever amounts you wish. Our daughter calls this a really yummy salad, and it goes over well if you take it to a dinner party or potluck.

Roasted squash, cut into bite-sized pieces

Green beans, cooked and chilled

1 can chickpeas, drained

1 cup arugula

Handful of dried cranberries

Kale, finely chopped

Celery, chopped

Curly-leaf parsley

Toasted pumpkin seeds

Vinaigrette of your choice

Toss all the ingredients in a large bowl. Dress with a light, slightly sweet vinaigrette.

Taco Salad

My friend Joyce shared this salad recipe with me long ago. It is easy and really makes a great supper salad.

1 lb lean ground beef

1 large onion, chopped

Chili powder

1 can red kidney beans

1 head of lettuce, chopped

1½ cup tomatoes, chopped

1 cup cheddar cheese, grated

1½ cup taco chips, broken

Kraft Russian dressing

Sour cream

Salsa

Sauté the meat, onions and chili powder until cooked, then cool. Add beans to the cooled chili.

Toss everything together with the dressing to taste. Serve with sour cream and salsa on the side.

Curried Chicken Salad

My friend Marion and I have used this salad many times for luncheons or light suppers. I serve it with steamed chilled asparagus, a wedge of lemon and butter-milk biscuits.

★ **Keep a container or two of pomegranate seeds in the freezer to use as a garnish. They're a treat for so many things!**

Cook, cool and chop the chicken. Toss together with the remaining salad ingredients in a large bowl and set aside.

In another bowl, stir dressing ingredients until thoroughly mixed. Combine salad and dressing and refrigerate for about an hour. Garnish with olives and parsley.

3 chicken breasts, boneless and skinless

1 nectarine, sliced

1 mango, sliced

4 green onions, chopped

½ red pepper, chopped

½ yellow pepper, chopped

2 apples, chopped

A handful of red grapes (organic if possible)

Toasted slivered almonds

DRESSING

½ cup mayonnaise

Glop of Sharwood's curry sauce, or a similar product

¼ cup mango chutney

1 tsp turmeric

2 tbsp sugar

2 tsp curry powder

2 tbsp lemon juice

1 tsp Dijon mustard

Pinch of salad seasoning

TOPPING

Black olives

Parsley

Naked Men

WE SIT, SIPPING steamy lattes, my friend and I, watching the world go by. Warm sun surrounds us at our wonderful spot on South Granville in Vancouver. She and I have been friends forever, though we've rarely lived in the same city and often not on the same continent. No matter, though: we have always stayed in contact, through births, deaths, marriage breakdowns and all the stuff in between.

My friend is single again, a widow this time, a merry widow in fact. She is looking for a new man or two, as many as she can find. Therefore, the topic of the day is men. She asks, "How many naked men have you seen?" We dissolve into helpless laughter. Such a crazy conversation at our age! But who cares? We are having fun.

"Let me tell you about the most interesting naked man I have ever seen," I say. She encourages me to proceed and sits back comfortably, spooning foam from her latte.

Here is the story: It is a beautiful early evening and Don and I have decided to walk over to a bistro not far from our condo. Crossing the road, we enter the tunnel under the Granville Street Bridge. I am aware of a slight sea breeze and the incredibly bright sunset to the west over the mountains. Musty summer smells greet us in the tunnel. Exiting, my eyes take a few seconds to become used to the dazzling light.

I stop in my tracks, gasp, take a few deep breaths, then regain my composure. I smile. About ten feet before us in the middle of the sidewalk is a man, completely naked. He is not in the bushes or even off to one side for privacy, but square in the middle of the walk we intend to use. Beside our naked neighbour are two piles of clothes—one his day wear and the other his evening attire, which he is changing into. With the man and his wardrobe in our way, we have to pass on the grass, through the goose droppings. As we go by, the well-muscled, naked gentleman bids us a good evening and we do likewise. It all feels so "Vancouver."

As I end my story, my friend carefully places her latte on the table and says, "Are you serious? You saw all of him?"

"Sure," I answer. "And he looked pretty darn good!"

Mystery Salad

Years ago, I had a salad that I loved in Holts Café in Edmonton. I believe they topped it with deep-fried noodles of some sort. This is my version.

Chicken breast

Clarified butter

A variety of greens

Green onions, chopped

Parsley, chopped

Red and yellow peppers, sliced

Asiago cheese, grated

DRESSING

3 tbsp undiluted frozen orange juice

Honey

Dijon mustard

Seasoning salt

Chopped fresh basil

Rice vinegar

Canola oil

Grill the chicken, using the clarified butter. While the chicken is cooking, toss the salad greens, onions, parsley and peppers in a large bowl. Add the dressing and toss.

Top with coarsely grated asiago cheese and serve with the grilled chicken.

Thursday Night Salad

I'm not sure why I named this Thursday Night Salad—we must have had it on a Thursday. But we really like it. As with many other recipes in this book, just use your own judgement on ingredient amounts.

Combine all salad ingredients except for the chicken, then combine the dressing ingredients. Toss together and serve with the chicken breast on top.

★ **To prepare the carrots, use a Japanese turning slicer (available at most specialty kitchen stores).**

Chicken breast, skinless, boneless and slow-roasted (1 per person)

Lettuce

Green onions, sliced

Sweet onion, sliced

Fresh mint

Red, yellow and orange peppers, cut in long fine strips

Orange slices

Cherry tomatoes

Celery, thinly sliced

Carrots, cut like vermicelli

Toasted sesame seeds, both white and black

DRESSING

Garlic, minced

Fresh ginger

Light soy sauce

Sesame oil, toasted

Rice vinegar

Canola oil

Sugar

Fresh orange juice

Orange rind

Mains

Dad's Flat Iron Steak

My dad cooked all his steaks this way. It is so yummy.

★ Chimichurri drizzled on the finished steak is really nice. Just mix finely chopped garlic, shallots and Italian parsley with oregano, salt and pepper, some good olive oil and a splash of vinegar. It should look like a dark green mish-mash when finished.

1 flat iron or flank steak

Garlic powder

Paprika

Salt and pepper

Coriander

Grapeseed oil

Ketchup

Worcestershire sauce

Pat the steak dry with paper towel, cut into serving-size pieces and cover with garlic powder, paprika, salt, pepper and coriander. Let rest for several hours.

Fast-fry the steak using grapeseed oil in a very good heavy-bottomed pan until medium-rare. (Grapeseed oil can take a higher heat than olive oil.) Remove to a platter and cover.

Pour a little water, ketchup, Worcestershire sauce and garlic powder in the pan and turn on high. Cook the sauce to desired consistency and pour over the steak.

Don's Short Ribs

THREE WAYS

I have to tell you, I almost never eat short ribs anymore (but only because they remind me of the night my beloved dog Ty died). Don, however, loves them—here are his favourite methods.

FIRST WAY

Beef short ribs

Salt and pepper

Brown sugar

Paprika

Vinegar

Garlic

Ketchup

Mustard

Worcestershire sauce

Cover ribs with the remaining ingredients. Cook, covered, for 3 hours at 300 degrees, then uncovered for 30 more minutes.

SECOND WAY

Steam or simmer the ribs until tender. Prepare the same ingredients as you did for the first way, then cover the ribs in the sauce and finish on the BBQ.

THIRD WAY

Beef short ribs

Onions

Garlic

Butter

Tomato paste

½ bottle red wine

Brown the ribs and remove from the pan. Sauté onions and garlic, add butter and some tomato paste and the wine. Place all the ingredients in a slow cooker for about 8 hours.

Letting Ty Go

PLEASE, NO. NOT NOW... I am not ready. Please, no. I love him so much.

Phone call... must do the right thing. Please, no.

I have prepared short ribs for dinner. I don't really like short ribs, but Don does and we are both really hurting.

Please no. Let him live. I start to bargain. I'll do anything.

We go to the vet hospital. The cold, harsh winter wind throws snow cruelly in every direction. I hardly notice.

Please, no. We hold him close one last time. He is so beautiful. Silky black fur, chocolate eyes full of love. Our first Belgian shepherd.

Please, no.

Yes. Release him. No more pain or suffering.

I am alone. He has gone.

Days pass. Where did we put the short ribs that sad evening, I wonder? On the roof of my car in the garage to cool. I forgot them there, I think, and they must have fallen off driving to the vet. I've lost food like that before.

Eighteen months later I am in the garage looking for something on a seldom used shelf. My hand finds something unexpected. There, pushed against the back of the shelf, is my wonderful green Emile Henry baking dish, intact with petrified ribs. I bring it inside and scrape the contents into the garbage. I clutch the pan and remember, and feel less alone.

Ten years have now passed, and the pain and loss have been replaced with gratitude and love. How very fortunate I was to learn a new kind of love through having Ty in my life. My heart fills with warmth and joy. I am not alone.

Roast Filet of Beef

I recently served three large filets at a party for sixty guests. It was terrific! Prepare a day ahead if you have time.

★ Use beef drippings from the oven pan and foil package to make a gravy. Just add red wine, finely chopped shallots and beef stock. Heat and reduce.

Filet of beef

Dijon mustard

Red wine

Garlic, crushed

RUB

Garlic powder

Roasted garlic powder

Paprika

Salt

Mignonette pepper (a lovely mix of tellicherry black pepper, white pepper and coriander)

Dry the roast with paper towel, then lightly rub with the mustard, wine and crushed garlic to coat. Make a dry rub with the remaining ingredients and cover the meat with it.

Wrap tightly and store in fridge overnight. Remove from fridge 1 hour prior to cooking.

Sear the roast on a very hot BBQ. Finish in a 375 degree oven, till just rare. Remove from the oven, wrap in foil and let sit for up to an hour if desired.

Shepherd's Pie

This pie is a great way to use left-over roast beef. Serve it with lots of veggies.

Roast beef

Garlic

Onion

Gravy and/or beef stock

Mashed potatoes

Put the roast in pieces through a food processor with the garlic, onion and a bit of watered-down gravy and beef stock. Process (don't over-process), put into a casserole dish, and top with mashed potatoes. Freeze and save it for one of those nights when you don't want to cook.

★ **Save and freeze separately some leftover gravy to top the shepherd's pie when you serve it.**

Chicken in Filo Pastry

This is a great recipe for entertaining. It can be made well ahead, wrapped individually and frozen. Thaw in the refrigerator and then bake. Serve with veggies and a salad, and maybe some nice rolls.

★ **At Christmastime, decorate this with red and green peppers.**

4 chicken breasts, boneless and skinless

¼ cup herbed cream cheese

1 roasted red pepper (from a jar)

8 leaves of spinach

4 sheets of filo

Butter, melted

Make a slit in the chicken and carefully stuff in some cheese, then a piece of pepper and finally a few spinach leaves. Wrap the chicken in filo, buttering between each layer—put on about 5 overlapping layers. Wrap in plastic wrap and freeze.

To serve, thaw in the refrigerator, remove plastic and bake at 350 degrees for about 1 hour, or until done.

Chicken Delicious

This is my version of a favourite item on the menu at our local bistro.

Place all of Part 1 in a food processor and process until the consistency is like a paste. Place in refrigerator for later use.

Combine Part 2 ingredients, and mix in a large skillet with first mixture, slowly heating through. Serve hot over Part 3: a pasta of your choice (I generally use linguini) and BBQ or baked chicken.

PART 1

3 cups sun-dried tomatoes, blanched in hot water for 3 minutes

10 cloves garlic, minced

½ cup toasted pine nuts

1 cup Parmesan, freshly grated

½ cup parsley

½ cup fresh basil

1 tbsp oregano

¾ cup virgin olive oil

PART 2

2 tbsp green peppercorns

1 tbsp capers

1 tbsp Italian seasoning

2 cups canned tomatoes

1 cup whipping cream

½ cup white wine (or more if needed to achieve the right consistency)

PART 3

Cooked chicken (BBQ or baked)

Pasta

Chicken Pot Pie

So many of these pies can be gummy. Not mine! The key to making a pie that isn't gummy is to use less sauce and more filling. Use your judgement for amounts: if after mixing the ingredients there is enough for two pies, so be it. Freeze one and bake the other.

★ When chopping the veggies, keep them large enough so that they are identifiable once the pie is cooked.

Good-quality boneless chicken breast, chopped into bite-sized pieces

White sauce (butter, flour and milk)

Carrots, cooked and chopped

Celery, cooked and chopped

Mushrooms, sautéed and sliced

Parsnips, cooked and chopped

Sweet onions, chopped and sautéed

Peas

Green onions, diced

Parsley, chopped

Pie pastry (see page 264)

Splash of white wine

Leftover gravy

Make your white sauce by sautéing equal amounts of butter and flour, then slowly stirring in milk and cooking gently until you have a thick sauce. Set aside.

Cook the chicken and sauté all of the vegetables. Place in a pie pan and pour over with your white sauce, then toss in a splash of white wine and some leftover gravy to give it a zing. Top with pie pastry and cook at about 375 degrees till the crust is golden.

Chicken Thighs

These are great to keep in the freezer.

6 chicken thighs, bone-in

1 tbsp red wine vinegar

1 tbsp olive oil

½ tsp fresh lemon juice

½ tsp Herbes de Provence

Pepper

Onion, in thick slices

Mix the vinegar, oil, lemon juice, herbs and pepper, and toss with the chicken. Arrange the chicken on onion slices. Pour remaining marinade overtop, then cook at 375 degrees for 50 minutes.

Tasty Coated Chicken

Serve this with your favourite dipping sauce, or a lemon sauce (fresh lemon juice, sugar, cornstarch and water, simmered till slightly thickened).

Chicken pieces

Marinade of your choice

3 egg whites

Cornstarch

Baking soda

Paprika

Vegetable oil, for cooking

Marinate chicken pieces in your favourite marinade for about an hour.

Beat egg whites in a bowl until frothy. In a separate dish, mix a large scoop of cornstarch with a spoonful of baking soda and lots of paprika.

Heat oil in a deep-frying pan on the stove. Dip each piece of chicken in egg whites, shake off the excess, then dip into the cornstarch mixture.

Brown chicken in oil on both sides, then transfer to baking pan. Bake at 350 degrees until cooked.

Taking Crazy on the Road

MANY WONDERFUL adventures occur "on the road" when we go to Don's office in Toronto. Toronto is a food and fashion mecca for me. I love it! I go every chance I get.

Before each trip I plan where we will eat and carefully research restaurants, food stores and cookbook stores. I do all my Christmas shopping in Toronto and come home with suitcases bulging.

I take the subway and streetcars, and I walk, learning where everything is—from the art gallery (which has a very good restaurant) to the shopping along Queen West. I head south on Yonge Street as far as St. Lawrence Market, then walk back east along King and Queen Streets. I find endless food shops, old warehouses with interesting stuff and great restaurants.

One night, we're having dinner at a lovely little bistro on Queen West and I try some chicken in a type of pastry I'd never seen. The next day I make it my business to track down what the pastry is and where I can get some. Kindly, the supplier takes my credit card over the phone and delivers a package of the pastry to our hotel, where it is stored in the hotel freezer until we are ready to leave. Upon checkout the front desk presents me with my pastry: a thirty-pound box of yufka. "What is this?" Don asks. "Oh, just some pastry…" We all love it for the year to follow.

Then there is the night we take clients to dinner at a fine restaurant, where they serve focaccia, warm on a slab of rough stone sitting on an iron stand heated by a candle. I love it and think it would be perfect in my home at our own dinner parties. But how to get it home? The restaurant has lots… perhaps they will sell me one of theirs? They do, and now I use my stone all the time.

One spring prior to Easter, as we head for the airport to return home, Don notices that my luggage is very heavy and asks what I've packed. "Oh, just some new potatoes for our Easter dinner." Shocked, he says, "But you can buy potatoes in Alberta!"

"Yes," I say. "But these are new baby potatoes!"

On another trip, I am worried we won't get a proper meal on Air Canada so I go to the St. Lawrence Market and buy some wonderful food to make filled buns. To keep the buns cool I wrap them in plastic bags and fill the hotel sink with ice. Don arrives back from a meeting and asks where he is supposed to brush his teeth. "Oh, use the bathtub," I advise. "That's lunch in the sink." Later, on our flight, the attendant notices our lunch and brings us a free bottle of champagne.

Each and every trip to Toronto we have a unique adventure. We also enjoy food shopping at home in the West and down the coast to Seattle. When we're in Calgary, I love The Cookbook Co. Cooks—another food lover's delight!

Chicken Stir Fry with Veggies and Noodles

Yum! A Friday night favourite.

Chicken, boneless

Egg noodles

Peanut oil

Ginger, grated

Garlic, grated

Carrots, cut into matchsticks

Celery, sliced thin on the diagonal

Cabbage, thinly sliced

Pea pods

Broccoli florets

SAUCE

¾ cup chicken broth

4 tbsp soy sauce

3 tbsp rice wine

2 tbsp sugar

2 tbsp cornstarch

Toasted sesame oil

Poach the chicken, then cube it and set aside. Cook the egg noodles in salted water. Sauté the veggies in peanut oil.

Mix the sauce ingredients together. When the noodles are al dente, drain, add sauce and chicken, and stir fry.

Lemon Chicken

Serve this with a pre-made lemon sauce—you can get it at Asian grocery stores. Or you can make a simple lemon sauce yourself (see the recipe headnote for Tasty Coated Chicken on page 141).

Chicken breasts (uniform size, flattened)

1 egg

Buttermilk

Onion powder

Garlic powder

Panko crumbs

Paprika

Salt and pepper

Seasoning salt

Chili powder (optional)

Grapeseed oil

Beat an egg with a little buttermilk and the onion and garlic powders. In a separate bowl, combine panko with paprika, pepper and salts, plus a little more onion and garlic powder.

Dip the chicken in the egg mixture, then coat in the seasoning mix. Fry the chicken, browning both sides in grapeseed oil. Finish in the oven.

Szechuan Chicken

This is a really good and easy chicken dish. We made it at Lake Muskoka once and, after dinner, put the bones out with the garbage. The next morning, the garbage was scattered every-where. Apparently during the night, the raccoons got into the garbage and enjoyed a dinner of their own. When we sat down to breakfast, we saw and smelled a raccoon at the cottage door. The smell was garlic, big time.

About 12 chicken thighs

1 bottle of VH Medium Garlic Rib Sauce

8 to 10 garlic cloves, chopped

2 tbsp fresh ginger

2 tbsp cornstarch

4 tbsp brown sugar

Mix the marinade ingredients and gently cook until boiling. Pour over about a dozen chicken thighs and bake at about 375 degrees until cooked (about 40 minutes). If you wish, you can finish off under the broiler to crisp and brown the chicken.

★ **I usually serve this dish with steamed broccoli and rice.**

Lamb Kebobs

These skewers can be formed ahead of time, making them great for a party.

Ground lamb

1 small egg

Onion, finely chopped

Garlic, finely chopped

Sumac

Coriander

Cumin

Allspice

Cayenne

Fresh ginger, grated

Pepper

Lemon juice

Mint, chopped

Mix all ingredients together, using amounts to taste. Form the mixture into sausage-like skewers and barbecue.

Leg of Lamb Roast

We always had leg of lamb at Easter, followed with a wonderful chocolate cake, decorated with a variety of colourful Easter eggs and served with ice cream on the side.

★ **Lamb is cooked when a meat thermometer reads at least 145 degrees. The exception is ground lamb, which should be cooked until it reaches 170 degrees to be well-done.**

Run the marinade ingredients through the processor and use two thirds of the mixture to coat the lamb. Leave the lamb to rest in the fridge for several hours.

Place in roasting pan with the remaining marinade. If you like, add some extra spices to taste, such as garlic powder, salt and pepper and paprika (I never do this the same way twice).

Roast at 425 to 450 degrees for 15 minutes, then reduce the heat to 140 degrees and finish cooking. Serve with sauce.

4 lb leg of lamb (bone removed)

MARINADE

5 to 6 cloves garlic

Oregano

Fresh mint leaves

2 tbsp chopped rosemary

Parsley, chopped

Pinch chili flakes

Olive oil

Lemon juice

SAUCE

½ cup red wine

2 tbsp apple jelly

1 cup chicken stock

1 tbsp balsamic vinegar

Best Ever Lamb Burgers

Serve these burgers with roasted garlic, soft goat cheese and a slice of heritage tomato on a soft brioche bun, or use your favourite combo.

★ **This lamb mixture can also be moulded onto wooden sticks and barbecued; or, omit the oregano and savory and add cumin, mint and any Moroccan spices you'd like. Serve the kebobs with a cool yogurt-type dip.**

1 lb ground lamb (I prefer Canadian)

1 onion, finely chopped

3 cloves garlic, minced

Splash of Tabasco

1 tsp oregano

1 tsp savory

Greek or lamb seasoning

Feta cheese

Condiments and burger fixings of your choice

Kaiser buns

Mix the lamb with the onion, garlic, Tabasco, oregano, savory and lamb seasoning. Form the lamb into patties and barbecue.

When the burgers are cooked, top with feta cheese on one side, and a combo of fresh tomato slices and bruschetta on the other.

Take some really good, soft kaiser buns and spread with garlic, basil, sun-dried tomato butter—any combination, your choice! Broil the buns until they are toasted and add the burgers.

Lamb Curry

I serve curry on nights I want an easy, tasty meal with no last-minute surprises or preparation. I would rate this as a "must keep" on my dinner party list. Most of the work is done the day before.

1 leg of lamb, cut into chunks (take the fat off)

Butter and/or oil

1 or 2 sweet onions, chopped

Several cloves garlic, chopped

1 red pepper, chopped

1 orange or yellow pepper, chopped

Several stalks of celery, chopped

1 head cauliflower, chopped

About 3 apples

A handful of dried apricots

Some flour (just enough to thicken the sauce)

About 500 ml organic chicken broth

1 can of coconut milk (organic if you can get it)

About half a jar of mango chutney

About 2 tbsp Madras curry paste (I use a medium from Fortnum & Mason)

Half a bottle of Sharwood's curry sauce

About 2 tbsp roasted ground cumin (I use Vij's)

Red pepper mix to taste (optional; I also use Vij's for this)

Sprinkle the meat with flour, brown it in a butter/oil combo, add the veggies and cook for a few minutes, then add the remaining ingredients.

The secret of a full-bodied, flavourful curry, in my opinion, is long slow cooking the day before it is served: a good rough estimate is about 2 to 3 hours in a 300-degree oven. Then cool it, put it in the fridge until the next day, and warm it in the oven. At serving time, transfer the lamb to a tagine pot, where it will remain warm.

I serve this with various chutneys, chopped nuts and yogurt. I also serve a carrot mash made the day before, plus rice and naan.

★ **I sometimes add two bags of Vij's Goan Lamb Curry to this—the addition gives the recipe some depth, and it's a good way to increase the recipe if you have extra guests or are running short of lamb.**

Lamb Shanks

TWO WAYS

These both make a hearty meal for a rainy night. Serve them with a cauliflower/potato mash and green salad.

FIRST WAY

4 lamb shanks

1 can roma tomatoes

1 large onion, chopped

8 cloves garlic, finely chopped

Rosemary

Fresh bay leaf

Oregano

Thyme

Salt and pepper

½ bottle red wine

1 can white beans

Combine all ingredients together and simmer on the stove until the lamb is done (see tip on page 146). When done, remove shanks and some tomatoes and beans to a serving dish and keep warm. Purée the remaining ingredients to make a sauce for the shanks.

SECOND WAY

4 lamb shanks

1 onion, chopped

3 cloves garlic, chopped

4 sprigs fresh rosemary

Fresh bay leaf

Oregano

Thyme

1 large can roma tomatoes

½ bottle wine (red or white)

Steam the shanks in a steam oven for 3 hours at 250 degrees (or 100% steam). After 3 hours, remove the shanks and place in a shallow pan with a lid. Place all the other ingredients in the pan around the shanks. Roast covered at 300 degrees for 1½ hours.

★ **If your sauce is too thick, add a little chicken stock or wine to thin it out.**

Lamb-Stuffed Pears

I have adapted this recipe from one of
my favourite books. I wanted a showstopper that I could make ahead and
freeze. I use pears most of the time,
but quince can work too. I use juice-
paste or jelly in the sauce.

★ **The pears must be firm or the recipe
will not work.**

2 lb ground leg of lamb

About 8 pears (you will need more
for the sauce)

2 garlic cloves, crushed

⅓ cup bread crumbs

Either a splash of red pepper sauce
or some red pepper flakes

⅔ tsp allspice

½ large sweet onion, finely chopped

1 egg

Ginger, grated

⅛ cup fresh mint, finely chopped

¼ cup Italian parsley, chopped

1 tbsp dried cilantro (optional)

SAUCE

1 tbsp olive oil

Onion, finely chopped

3 pears, peeled and finely chopped

2 tbsp quince jelly or paste

1 tbsp fresh lemon juice

1 piece ginger, grated

1 tsp cardamom

¼ tsp allspice

1 tbsp pomegranate syrup

3 cups chicken stock

GARNISH

Fresh mint, chopped

Pomegranate seeds

Mix all of the main ingredients except the pears and put in fridge.

Peel pears and cut in half. Place them in "fruit fresh" powder or coat in lemon juice to keep them from turning brown.

Make large balls of the lamb mixture with your hands and stuff it in the pear halves.

To make the sauce, sauté onions and pears in oil then add the remaining ingredients. Simmer for 10 minutes. Transfer the sauce to a large heavy-bottomed or stovetop-safe pan. It must be deep enough to hold the pears stuffed with lamb and be covered with a lid for the final cooking.

Simmer on the stovetop for 50 minutes or in the oven for about 45 minutes. Check the lamb using a thermometer—when it is 170 degrees, it is done.

When cooked, carefully transfer the stuffed pears into your serving dish and pour the sauce around them. Garnish with chopped fresh mint and sprinkle with pomegranate seeds.

This is very easy to freeze and reheat. If you wish to freeze the dish for later use, wait to add your garnish.

Kids Can Cook Too

OF COURSE KIDS CAN COOK. They are brilliant, fun and definitely up for the challenge. I have yet to meet a kid who does not enjoy cooking with a loving, patient adult.

As far back as I can remember I have been involved in food preparation and sharing meals with family and friends. At an early age, under the tutelage of my parents, my grandmother and my Aunt Ann, I was schooled in food preparation and the rituals that accompany it. To this day Aunt Annie's words ring in my ears: "Noni, mind your manners."

As an adult I have often involved children in cooking. One of my favourite photos is of Suzanne sitting on the counter mixing dough. She was about four years old. I still have Lisa's childlike handwritten recipes in a notebook. Today, both are excellent cooks and gracious hostesses.

Henry, Suzanne's three-year-old, often helps his mom as they prepare supper. He will proudly tell you how he makes pizza dough, then places on the toppings. Under his mother's direction, he chops ingredients for salads. Suzanne says the key to introducing new food into his diet is his participation in the preparation. She started Henry's cooking experience early: before he was even two, he was cracking eggs into a bowl.

Today when I hear adults say with pride and disdain, "Oh, I don't cook," I think that is a loss for them, and for their children.

Cooking with kids is fun! It teaches them teamwork, communication and planning; increases self-esteem and awareness of the environment; and instills the concept of respect for the fruits of people's labour. Most recipes in my book can be created with the participation of a child. It may take a little longer, but in the end you will have a confident, creative child interested in what they eat. And it creates lots of parent-child bonding time!

Lamb Tagine

Sauté the lamb chunks and sausage until browned. Add the remaining ingredients and simmer together in a tagine pot or Dutch oven for a long slow cook. Add and adjust ingredients as you wish.

★ **You can also substitute chicken for lamb.**

This is one of my favourite recipes. It's great for a crowd.

Lamb chunks, usually from the leg

Lamb sausage, ground and pressed into small balls

1 can unsalted tomatoes, chopped

1 or 2 tins chickpeas, washed

Ginger, minced

Garlic, minced

Onions, chopped

Tomato sauce

Carrots, chopped

Sweet potatoes, chopped

Squash, cubed

Turmeric

Cinnamon

Dates

Dried apricots

Cilantro

Rack of Lamb

THREE WAYS

This is a very special dish, so save it for your lamb-lover friends. We often enjoy it with Maggie and Paul on Pender Island. The third way has been kindly shared from Ian, who is the son of my friend Marion.

FIRST WAY

Lamb

Dijon mustard

Salt and pepper

Thyme

Rosemary

Red wine

SAUCE

1 shallot, finely chopped

3 cloves garlic, finely minced

½ cup red wine

¼ cup beef stock

Dry rack of lamb with paper towel. Rub with mustard and spices and a little red wine. Cook in the oven at 400 degrees for about 20 minutes, then reduce heat until done. Use a meat thermometer— the temperature should be no lower than 130 degrees. You might like to finish by adding 1 tbsp butter.

Combine sauce ingredients, and pour over lamb.

SECOND WAY

Prepare as with the first way, but use a dry rub of garlic powder, salt and pepper, coriander, paprika and oregano. For this method, let stand for a couple of hours in the fridge after applying the rub.

THIRD WAY

First, rub the racks with oil, salt and pepper, garlic, thyme and rosemary. Then brown in a pan and transfer to the oven to finish cooking at 375 degrees until a meat thermometer reaches 130 degrees.

Prepare a gravy, using a generous blob of butter, 2 tbsp Dijon mustard, 1 tbsp grainy mustard, ½ cup maple syrup and some Herbes de Provence. Serve with mashed potatoes, carrots and beets or asparagus.

Stuffed Leg of Lamb

My mom always stuffed her boned leg of lamb and served it with her own mint sauce, which was a combo of the store stuff and fresh mint.

1 butterflied leg of lamb

1 lb ground lamb

3 Greek lamb sausages

Red onion, chopped

Shallots, chopped

Garlic, minced

2 eggs

Bread crumbs

Fresh mint

Thyme

Oregano

Cumin

Turmeric

Dates

Dried apricots

Cook all of the lamb fully and set aside. Then, sauté the onion, shallots and garlic.

In a large bowl, combine the meat with the veggies. Add eggs, bread crumbs, herbs, spices and dried fruit. Press the stuffing into the butterflied leg of lamb and tie. Roast until your meat thermometer reads 125 to 130 degrees.

Baked Ham

TWO WAYS

FIRST WAY

1 pre-cooked ham

1 can of beer

Fresh bay leaves

Whole cloves

Onion

Mustard powder

Brown sugar

Bake ham, covered, for 2 to 3 hours in a low oven (300 degrees) with beer, bay leaves, cloves and onion.

Remove the ham from the oven and peel off the skin and fat. Glaze with dry mustard, brown sugar and more cloves. Return to the oven and bake for another 20 to 30 minutes at 400 degrees.

★ **Baked ham can be so wonderful, or it can be salty—know your butcher! I find the can of beer helps reduce any excess salty flavour.**

SECOND WAY

1 pre-cooked ham

Mustard powder

Brown sugar

Garnish of your choice

Rub the ham with a mixture of dry mustard and brown sugar. I decorate it with pineapple rings, whole cloves and maraschino cherries, all held in place with toothpicks. Vary the fruit as you like.

Bake until the ham is warm through.

The first way is simply a delicious way to prepare ham. This second is also wonderful—it is similar to how my mom used to prepare hers. After my mother's memorial service, I served baked ham, salad, curried fruit bake, buns, pickles and mustards—an easy, do-ahead menu. It smelled so good coming into the house after the memorial service. People came and went and helped themselves to the buffet.

Endings

I WAS ABOUT FIVE YEARS OLD when I attended my first funeral. It was for Grandfather R.J. As Dr. Ramsey spoke of his old, dear friend, tears streamed down his worn face. No friend could ever have loved another more. I was mesmerized, and have carried the memory of that service since.

Now I find myself being dubbed "the funeral planner" by my friends. The responsibility of this duty has fallen on me as the only family member young enough to take on the work. Planning a funeral or memorial service is a two-part procedure: before the gathering and sharing of food, first you must plan the service in some sort of formal way. I did this for my dad's funeral, often working through the order of the service with the minister.

I chose to visit a large nursery rather than a florist, feeling I'd get a better bang for my buck. I ordered twenty large baskets of trailing, tangerine-coloured impatiens to be delivered to the church the day of the memorial service. The front of the church had different levels, and the flowers made a stunning waterfall of colour.

My father was an avid gardener, so flowers were quite appropriate. At the end of the service, friends were invited to remember Dad by taking one of the baskets to enjoy in their garden for the summer.

I was shocked when my shy, then fifteen-year-old daughter asked to speak at the memorial service. I agreed as long as she would practice prior to the event, which she did. She was amazing. She spoke lovingly of my dad's love and support, then went on to read from Kahlil Gibran on death. She closed with "Where the Sidewalk Ends" by Shel Silverstein.

It was a really wonderful service, followed by one of my funeral buffets. Guests were invited to return to our home, where the aroma of good food greeted them as they entered. The menu included baked ham with mustard sauce, pickles and olives; warm curried fruit; tossed salad; raw veggies; soft buns and breads; cookies and squares; wine, juice, tea and coffee.

Rituals such as memorial services provide an opportunity to honour the memory of the deceased and celebrate their life, while helping us process our pain, loss and grief. These rituals give us the time and space we need for healing and transformation. We are a people of beginnings and endings. Living through both pain and joy is an essential part of our life's journey.

Pork Lettuce Wraps

Peanut oil

Ground pork (or chicken or turkey)

Garlic, chopped

Ginger, finely chopped

Shallots, chopped

Onions, chopped

Carrots, finely chopped

Celery, chopped

Cabbage, chopped

Green onions, chopped

Cremini mushrooms, chopped

Water chestnuts, chopped

Red pepper, chopped

Hoisin sauce

Sherry

Toasted sesame oil

Lettuce, for presenting

In a large frying pan, combine the ingredients and cook. Drain off fat, return to pan and finish off. Serve hot, wrapped in chilled lettuce leaves. Butter lettuce works nicely.

These are so good for a light supper. The ingredients and amounts are flexible—start with mine as a guide, or make them how you like.

Maggie's Sweet and Sour Pork

1 lb pork tenderloin

1 tbsp sherry

2 tbsp light soy sauce

2 tbsp flour

1 tbsp cornstarch

Canola oil

3 peppers (a mix of colours)

1 large sweet onion, chopped

Several carrots, thinly sliced

1 small tin bamboo shoots

2 cups pea pods

Several wedges of pineapple

SAUCE

6 tbsp sugar

4 tbsp soy sauce

1 tbsp sherry

2 tbsp vinegar

4 tbsp tomato sauce or ketchup

½ tbsp cornstarch mixed with ½ cup water

I love this recipe. My friend Maggie shared it with me years ago when she first moved from the UK to Canada. The original hand-written recipe is covered in blobs of who knows what, so I have made some changes and updates.

Cut the pork and mix well with the sherry, soy, flour and cornstarch. Sauté in the oil until golden, then remove from pan and keep warm.

Sauté the vegetables and pineapple in a little canola oil. Mix the sauce ingredients until smooth, then combine with the meat and veggies in the pan. Stir constantly until cooked. Serve with rice.

My Pork Ribs

These are great served with a large salad and garlic bread (see page 55).

★ **An alternate way to cook this would be in a steam convection oven for about 1 hour; finish on the barbecue.**

About 4 strips of pork ribs, lean and meaty

Onions, chopped

Garlic, chopped

Chicken stock

Pepper

Your favourite dry rub

Sauce of your choice

Simmer the ribs in a large pot with the other ingredients for a couple of hours. When tender, remove from the pot and cover with garlic powder, salt and pepper, or a rub of your choice. Barbecue until nicely browned, then add your favourite sauce and finish them off.

Lou's Purple Cabbage

One of Lou's best menus is a shoulder roast of pork, covered in crackling, served with gravy, roast veggies and her famous purple cabbage. It is so good with any pork meal.

2 slices of bacon

A bit of butter

1 onion, chopped

1 large apple, chopped

1 medium purple cabbage, chopped

About 3 tbsp brown sugar

A good splash of apple cider vinegar

Sauté the bacon, adding the butter, onion, apple and cabbage. Cook for a bit, then add the remaining ingredients. Cover and cook at a low temperature for about 2 hours.

A Strange Way to Meet a Friend

SOMETIMES OUT OF tragedy comes something good. After a heavy rain, the sky clears, the sun pops out and the air has that warm post-rain feel typical of Vancouver. Misha and I stroll across the street into our park for our last outing of the day.

Suddenly the still evening is shattered by a crashing noise and what sounds like an explosion. I look up to see a huge semi-truck floating through the air, falling from the east on-ramp of the Granville Street Bridge down on to West Fourth Avenue below. There are a few seconds of silence as the truck falls, then it lands with a bang on its side.

I stand in utter shock. How can this happen? The whole park freezes and it is totally quiet until the silence is broken by distant sirens. Within minutes, police, fire trucks and ambulances appear. It is amazing how quickly first responders mobilize and onlookers gather.

As I stand glued to my spot on the grass, I realize I am wearing ugly torn sport shorts and a ratty old t-shirt… the plan was that no one in the park would see me on this quick trip out with my dog. But as luck would have it, I hear a voice beside me: "Hi, I am your neighbour, Louise."

And that was the beginning of a long and wonderful friendship with Lou.

Tourtière

Every Christmas, we have tourtière, sometimes on Christmas Eve. The spice amounts often need adjusting as you cook, so just use your judgement—but use lots, tasting as you go.

1½ lb ground pork

1 cup chicken broth

1 medium onion, chopped

Several cloves garlic, finely chopped

1 potato, mashed

1 egg, beaten

Dry mustard

Thyme

Sage

Allspice

Cloves

Marjoram

Pastry (see page 264)

Combine the pork, chicken broth, onions and garlic in a large frying pan. Cook for about 25 minutes. Drain off the fat and add the mashed potato, egg and spices. Cook until finished, then place in pie pan and cool.

Top with a pastry of your choice (I do not use a bottom crust).

Bake at 425 degrees for about 20 minutes.

Chili Prawns

12 prawns, thawed

4 cloves garlic, finely chopped

2 tbsp paprika

Freshly ground black pepper, to taste

4 tbsp dried onion flakes

Butter, for frying

2 cups steamed Asian greens,
such as bok choy or gai lan

SAUCE

1 tbsp ginger, minced

Hot chili sauce

2 tbsp sugar

2 tbsp light soy sauce

2 tbsp rice vinegar

2 tbsp hoisin sauce

¼ cup chicken stock

¼ cup ketchup

2 tbsp sherry

I first had these at a restaurant in Edmonton. This is my version. I like to buy my prawns frozen from the fish market on Granville Island, where they are large and flavourful. Apparently, they are quick-frozen at sea as soon as they are caught, making them as fresh as possible. I find the thawed ones in the case can look quite dreary sometimes.

Combine the garlic and spices and rub on the prawns. Refrigerate for about 1 hour.

Heat the sauce ingredients on stove; simmer for a few minutes, and keep warm while you cook the prawns in butter. When cooked, place them on a bed of freshly steamed greens and drizzle the sauce overtop.

★ Thawing frozen prawns takes almost no time. Just take what you need out of the bag and put them in a colander under cold running water. They will be usable in about two or three minutes.

Prawn Perfection

I love this stuff—I serve it over pasta. The prawns must be large and of really good quality. I buy mine frozen in a three-pound bag at the fish market, only thawing slightly under cold running water before cooking.

Lots of prawns

Clarified butter

1 tsp tarragon

1 tsp oregano

1 tsp basil

1 tsp thyme

¼ tsp sage

¼ tsp marjoram

White wine

1 tbsp onion, finely diced

Several cloves garlic, minced

2 tbsp Worcestershire sauce

½ tsp hot sauce

Juice of half a lemon

Lemon rind

Tomatoes

Spinach

Simmer the tarragon, oregano, basil, thyme, sage and marjoram in lots of clarified butter, then add a splash of wine. Once that's simmered, add the onion, garlic, Worcestershire, hot sauce and lemon juice and rind. Set aside.

Sauté the prawns in butter (with some garlic and onions, if you like). When nearly cooked, add fresh-cut tomatoes, spinach and the spice mixture. Keep at a low temperature until ready to serve.

★ **Before cooking prawns, put them on their back and make two incisions on their underside. This helps straighten them.**

Seafood Curry

This curry is just wonderful for entertaining! So much can be done ahead. I love serving this meal on Christmas Eve. Everyone helps in the preparation, under Lisa's guidance.

About 1 lb uncooked prawns

2 cups scallops

2 cups crabmeat

1 or 2 lobster tails (optional)

Clarified butter

SAUCE

3 tbsp clarified butter

A handful of flour

Curry powder

2 cloves garlic, minced

1 shallot, minced

A handful of grated asiago cheese

Splash of brandy

½ cup white wine

2 tbsp tomato paste

1 cup cream

Thaw the seafood in the fridge, then cook each separately—all but the lobster can be sautéed in clarified garlic butter. If you are using lobster, it should be steamed. When the seafood is cooked, cool and refrigerate.

Combine the sauce ingredients and cook. (This sauce can be made ahead and kept in the fridge until serving time.) When you are ready to serve, combine the seafood and sauce, warming slowly. I serve it with a good pasta and top it with Italian parsley.

Sea Scallops

I serve these with pasta and a simple green salad.

★ **Soak scallops in milk to get rid of any sand and grit.**

1 lb frozen scallops

Salt and pepper

Paprika

Flour, for coating

Grapeseed oil

Dry white wine

Dijon mustard

Cream

Shallots, minced

Thaw the scallops and thoroughly pat dry with paper towel. Season and dust with a very light coating of flour, then sauté in grapeseed oil until golden. Remove scallops from pan.

To the same pan, add dry wine, mustard, cream and shallots. Return the scallops to the pan, heat thoroughly and serve.

Simple Salmon
THREE WAYS

After trying all kinds of recipes for salmon, I am back to my favourite three ways. These are all so easy, and if you want to dress the fish up after it is cooked, do.

★ Cold, baked salmon is great in sandwiches or salad.

FIRST WAY

1 beautiful BC salmon filet

Lemon

Butter

Place salmon on foil and top with slices of lemon. Wrap the foil around the salmon like a package and bake on a cookie sheet in a hot oven for about 15 to 20 minutes, depending on the thickness. Enjoy with lemon juice and melted butter.

SECOND WAY

4 small salmon filets, skin removed

Balsamic vinegar

Maple syrup

Dijon mustard

Combine wet ingredients and coat salmon. Sauté both sides. Finish in the oven.

THIRD WAY

1 salmon filet

Dill

Lemon

Place a trivet or some foil bunched up into a doughnut shape on the bottom of a heavy saucepan. Place some dill, lemon and water in the bottom. Place the salmon on top and gently poach, covered. Top with lemons and fresh dill. Serve warm with a sauce of your choice, or chill and serve with salad.

Catching Crab

IT IS THE SUMMER of 2017 and Mikah and his mom Nicole are visiting Pender Island. It is his first visit in three years and so it is a very special time for our whole family.

Mikah remembers catching crabs off our dock and is keen to test his luck, so off we all go to the dock with two crab traps. Don and Mikah have the remains of some fish they caught the previous day to use as bait.

Don and Mikah place heads and tails into the traps, then toss them off the dock into the sea. After about twenty minutes, the traps are pulled up with several crabs.

However, getting the crabs out of the traps is the true adventure, and provides for gales of laughter. These crabs are determined not to be supper. One hilarious moment has Don yelling in pain as he yanks his arm out of the trap, with a very angry crab attached to his finger. The crab lets go and flies through the air, only to be quickly caught by Mikah's gloved hand.

Little Henry, our three-year-old grandson, watches wide-eyed.

Supper is amazing, with a little additional halibut topped with fresh butter and accompanied by garden asparagus and lots of lemon.

Crab Cakes

Only make these if good-quality fresh crab is available. Dungeness crab flavour is easily lost if over-handled or frozen.

Fresh cooked crab

Bread crumbs (soft)

Grapeseed oil

Mayonnaise

1 egg, beaten

Lemon juice

Dijon mustard

Thyme

Worcestershire sauce

Tabasco or other hot sauce

Red pepper, finely chopped

Celery, finely chopped

Paprika

Mix all the condiments together. Gently take bread crumbs and mix together in a large bowl. Add only enough of the sauce to bind the cakes.

Gently mould crab mixture into cakes. Do not overwork! Place on a cooking tray in the fridge for an hour, then fry in grapeseed oil.

Pickerel

Fresh pickerel is amazing! It is available fresh in Alberta.

Pickerel filets

Butter

Shallots, minced

Capers

White wine

Sauté filets with the rest of the ingredients. Top with toasted almonds.

★ **Try this with brown butter.**

Veggies and Sides

Preparing Vegetables

Today, many complicated recipes are available for veggie preparation, and often they are quite tasty. However, my first choice for serving vegetables is to keep it simple. There is nothing more wonderful and healthy than freshly picked organic or market-purchased veggies, steamed and served in an unadulterated form, allowing their natural flavours to shine. Here are some of the herbs, oils and spices I use with various vegetables.

★ Harissa, oil and lemon juice is also a nice combination for roasted veggies.

Asparagus Butter, lemon, cheese.

Beans Butter, salt and pepper, Asian flavours, chili peppers.

Beets Butter, salt and pepper, balsamic vinegar, sugar or honey, dill, garlic, goat cheese, orange juice, lemon juice, shallots, walnuts, sour cream.

Broccoli Butter, fresh lemon juice, cheese sauces, chili pepper, garlic, Asian sauces.

Brussels Sprouts Butter, salt and pepper, sugar, hazelnuts, bacon or pancetta, cider vinegar, garlic, balsamic vinegar, maple syrup, walnuts.

Cabbage Sugar, apples, vinegars, bacon, chestnuts.

Carrots Butter, peppers, sugar, salt and pepper, orange juice, cumin, maple syrup, Asian sauces.

Cauliflower Butter, lemon juice, cheese sauces, Asian spices.

Chard Butter, sugar, garlic, lemon juice, onion.

Corn Butter, salt and pepper, sweet basil, curry powder, onions.

Fava Beans Any of the stronger cheeses, garlic, parsley, thyme, savory. Puréed fava beans make wonderful dips.

Kohlrabi Butter, some cheeses, mustard, garlic, soy sauce, sesame oil.

Potatoes Butter, salt and pepper, cheeses, chives, sour cream, bacon, parsley, garlic, rosemary.

Sauerkraut Apples, bacon, brown sugar, sausages, white vinegar.

Snap Peas Olive oil, finish with sea salt, pepper, toasted almonds.

Spinach Butter, salt and pepper, sugar, red wine vinegar, dill, cream sauces, cheese (such as feta and ricotta), mint, lemon juice, Asian sauces, balsamic vinegar.

Squash Butter, salt and pepper, sugar, maple syrup, sage, garlic, olive oil, onions, thyme.

Summer Squash (Zucchini) Basil, cheeses, salt and pepper, peppers, parsley, oils.

Tomatoes Salt and pepper, oregano, sugar, thyme, basil, cheeses, peppers, lemon juice, balsamic vinegar, olive oil, parsley, green onion, fennel pollen, tarragon.

Turnips Salt and pepper, butter, sugar, apples, garlic, marjoram, parsley, thyme.

Garlicky Green Beans

Good, fresh green beans are one of the greatest veggies.

Green beans

Lots of garlic, grated

Oil

Red pepper, chopped

Slivered almonds, toasted

Trim, blanch and drain the beans, then set aside.

Sauté the garlic in oil and lightly cook the peppers. And add to the drained beans and top with the almonds.

Barley Casserole

This dish is a nice side for chicken, pork or lamb.

⅓ cup barley

Splash of olive oil

1 small sweet onion, finely chopped

1 clove garlic, finely chopped

1½ cups cubed squash

1 tsp dried thyme

4 cups chicken stock

¼ cup white wine

Parmesan, grated

Rinse barley and set aside. Sauté onion, garlic and squash in oil. Transfer to a casserole dish and cover with remaining ingredients. Cook at 375 degrees for 50 minutes. Top with Parmesan and serve.

Grilled Veggies

These are great for your backyard barbecue.

Any veggies you have on hand

Oil

Balsamic vinegar

Maple syrup

Fresh thyme

Savory

Salt and pepper

Mix the veggies with vegetable oil of your choice and the rest of the ingredients. Grill to taste!

★ **A great combination is asparagus, peppers, red onions, carrots and zucchini.**

Lisa's Roasted Onions

My daughter Lisa serves these with beef.

4 large onions

1 tbsp olive oil

⅓ cup good balsamic vinegar

¼ tsp salt

Slice the tops off the onions and peel, leaving the root end. Cut each onion into eight wedges, pour the oil and vinegar mixture over and bake at 450 degrees until tender. Salt to taste.

Backyard Fish

"**D**OUBLE, DOUBLE TOIL** and trouble; Fire burn, and cauldron bubble."

I am reminded of Shakespeare's *Macbeth*, Act 4, scene i, as I watch my husband tend his cauldron of bubbling water, sitting on a large burner, on our deck beside the pond. "What are you doing?" I ask. "Warming the pond water. It needs to come up to twenty degrees," he responds. Today is the day the fish leave their indoor home for the pond in our backyard vegetable garden.

It all began about a dozen years ago, long before water features were in vogue. First we collected information pertaining to water gardens. Next we dug a large hole, lined it and filled it with water. Finally, we surrounded our new pond with rocks and plants. Using a series of larger rocks, we created a "stepped" water course, which provided aeration for the pool and has a wonderful audiovisual effect. At night, the pond is illuminated by an underwater floodlight.

One day, sitting by the pond and feeling joy and relief at the completion of the project, I look up to see my husband proudly standing above me. "Look what I've got," he says, thrusting a small plastic bag filled with water toward me. Oddly, the water appears to be moving—with twenty-five assorted feeder goldfish, very tiny, about the length of a small fingernail. And so our lives with our fish begin.

We are new to fish, and not aware that the water must be specially treated. We kill about nine before purchasing neutralizer to make the water safe for our new pets. The remaining fish survive and flourish through the summer.

Autumn arrives. Soon the cool breezes of early October warn us that winter is coming. "What about the fish?" we ask ourselves. Home is in Edmonton—not the best place to over-winter fish outdoors. The books we've consulted are written for warmer climates. Whoops! Well-meaning folk advise us to leave them in the pond over the winter, assuring us it is deep enough and the fish will probably survive. "Probably" is not good enough for my husband, who by now has bonded with the fish.

One of my spouse's endearing qualities is that he always has a solution. "No problem," he says. "We will buy a hard plastic pond liner at a garden shop, place it in the living room in a corner, and surround it with plants. "No, no!" I moan. "Wouldn't the basement be a better location?" Patiently he explains: "The fish need the living room light. They will be a conversation piece. Don't worry, it will be wonderful!" I am not convinced, but in they come with all their equipment, including the ugly, rigid black liner filled with water and now not-so-small fish. Don surrounds the liner with plants, all sitting on my glistening hardwood floor, protected only by an area rug. Amazingly, we all survive the winter. When they return to the backyard in the spring, no harm has come to the house.

Silly me! "Wouldn't a few frogs be fun?" I suggest. Yes, Don just happens to know of some kids who like catching tadpoles.

Soon we are the fortunate owners of a bunch of tadpoles that become frogs. It is a mystery to me, but pools of fish seem to connect with some primitive male part in a very positive way. One benefit of the fishpond is how wonderfully it can quiet an unhappy man, rendering him gentle. Happiness is a pond full of multicoloured fish. Just ask my husband.

When winter again looms, we prepare to bring our little friends and all their paraphernalia back into the living room. But the weather changes suddenly, and we have to net the fish and frogs late at night in the dark. Some weeks later, the dogs start acting agitated around one living room chair. We look behind the chair and find ourselves staring sadly down at a dead frog. Dead frog number two is behind the pond, along with a small leak.

When spring comes, I find my voice. "Enough," I declare. "Next winter the fish go to the basement, so start planning now!" And so Don does. A trip to the country and he comes back with a 100-gallon cattle trough, grow lights, plants and even a few bugs that are flying around the plants. Today, we have nine very large fish in the pond—the originals plus one baby born two summers ago, and no frogs at this time. Our wintering pond in the basement is a complete ecosystem, and all can exist in total harmony. More importantly, I have the living room back!

Roasted Beets

Beets are one of my favourite vegetables. They can be made ahead and rewarmed.

★ **In early summer, beets are lovely served on top of their greens. Don't overcook the beet greens—just steam them until they wilt.**

8 medium-sized beets (a mix of colours)

Cinnamon

Sugar

Ground cloves

½ cup white wine

1 fresh bay leaf

2 chopped shallots

1 clove garlic, minced

Peel the beets, then sprinkle a tiny pinch each of cinnamon, sugar and cloves overtop. Add 1 cup of water and the rest of the ingredients. Put the entire mixture in a large baking dish and cover tightly with foil. Bake for about 1 hour at 350 degrees or until tender.

After cooking, drain the beets. Add butter, salt and pepper to taste.

Parsnips

TWO WAYS

Pretty much whatever you do with carrots, you can do with parsnips. I cut them into sticks. I like mixing the two veggies and adding a small amount of butter, a pinch of sugar and salt and pepper to taste.

★ **I really like parsnips finished in brown butter.**

FIRST WAY

Cut parsnips into chunks and parboil. Do not overcook. Drain and dry. Sauté in a little butter and oil to brown them slightly. Top with toasted almonds and some finely chopped parsley and chives.

SECOND WAY

Cut parsnips into chunks (core if necessary), then steam, drain and sauté in butter and maple syrup. Top with sea salt.

Mustardy Brussels Sprouts

A crowd-pleasing way to prepare Brussels sprouts.

½ cup balsamic vinegar

¼ cup olive or grapeseed oil

2 tbsp sugar

2 tbsp Dijon mustard

Salt

Mix balsamic, oil, sugar, Dijon and salt to taste and coat your sprouts. Bake on a tray at 350 degrees for 30 minutes. Top with crumbled bacon if you wish.

Yellow Beets with Brussels Sprouts and Grapes

This is a delicious and beautiful combination of colours and flavours.

Yellow beets

Brussels sprouts

Red seedless grapes, whole

Butter

Balsamic vinegar

Sugar

Salt and pepper

Cut the beets into chunks and the Brussels sprouts in half, then steam both. Add remaining ingredients and toss.

Val's Cabbage Rolls

This recipe comes from my friend Val, who is an amazing cook. She makes her rolls with sour cabbage from a farm stand outside of Edmonton—they are truly wonderful.

1 large head sour cabbage

1½ cups dry rice (white, sticky or brown, your choice)

Several onions, chopped

Butter

Place sour cabbage in a bowl and cover with boiling water. Rinse really well several times and gently begin separating the leaves. Be sure to rinse the salt off.

Cook the rice and sauté the onions separately and let cool. Combine once cooled.

Cut the cabbage leaves in half if large. Place a spoonful of rice/onion mixture on the triangle; fold the first corner over the filling, then the bottom edge, then the next corner and roll away from you.

Use any leftover leaves to line the bottom of your pan. Place the rolls tightly in the pan, then add ¾ cup of water and top with a few dollops of butter. Cover and bake at about 325 degrees for approximately 2 hours or longer.

Loss of a Car,
Raspberries and Integrity

IT IS A BEAUTIFUL, warm, sunny August morning. We leave the Trout Lake Farmers' Market in Vancouver, heavily laden with beautiful peaches, large fragrant raspberries and veggies.

Tomorrow we plan to drive with our dog Misha to Calgary, where I will make raspberry jam and share the produce with our children. We carefully place our treasures in the back of my Jeep. Heading along Victoria Drive, we approach Twelfth Avenue—the light is green, so we enter the intersection… and then it happens. I feel and hear a loud explosion, like a bomb going off. The Jeep starts to spin in what feels like slow motion, then the tipping starts. I wonder: can the vehicle right itself? *No*… Over we go, peaches flying everywhere, raspberries splatting on the windows. We are on our side. My right ear and cheek are on the pavement.

It registers—we have just had a major accident. Don and I are both conscious and trapped in seatbelts in a smoking car.

Don finally gets his belt undone and, with help from strangers, gets out the back. I am to be next, however, I am not in any hurry to leave. I feel not too bad—I am still alive, but I don't know the condition of my spine and I am not willing to let just anyone haul me up and out. I am unaware of the danger of the smoking car. Meanwhile,

Don is threatening to go back in and get me if someone doesn't convince me I have to be removed. Fortunately a doctor comes along, and she talks me up and out with the help of medics.

Both Don and I are placed on spine boards. We are awaiting transport to Vancouver General Hospital when the driver of the car who ran the red light walks over and takes full responsibility for the accident. I am truly moved by the integrity and courage it took for him to come to us as we're lying on the road. I wonder what I might have done had we been responsible for harming someone. I hope that I would do what was right.

In the ambulance I try to phone Suzanne on someone's cell, but my hands are shaking too badly. Eventually, when we're in the ER in the hospital, I get her. Suzanne is our take-charge daughter. Lisa is our gentle soul, so kind and helpful. Both have worked in the medical field and know their way around hospitals, as do I.

Within moments of my phone call, I am being social worked. After many trips to x-ray and lots of attention, the waiting begins—you know, "hospital waiting." The social worker has pretty much shared her life story with me, and I am getting restless and ready to be off this damn spine board. But how will I make it happen? Easy. I tell the social worker I am going to vomit. Well, that brings the nurses and doctors running. They don't want the patient—me—aspirating. I am off the spine board in seconds. Good, now I want out.

I haven't seen Don since we left the road. I later learn that his nurse, a dear man named Orin, came running into his room and said, "They are all coming. Your daughters." He tells us they are on an Air Canada flight and are due in half an hour.

"Well, Orin," Don told him, "it would be in your best interest to get us out of here before they land." So we are discharged and told to take it easy. I no longer have a Jeep but we seem not too bad, all things considered, and glad to be alive.

Three years and many lawyer visits later we are ready to settle the lawsuit. Before proceedings officially begin, I ask if I may speak. Everyone seems surprised but I'm told I may.

"I would like to thank Mr. Brown for having the courage and integrity to come over to our destroyed car and possibly wrecked lives and apologize. We both really appreciated it, so thank you."

With that, the proceedings started and I learn that Mr. Brown has changed his mind. He denied, in a prior statement, running the red light and attempted to place the blame on us. Fortunately, there were many witnesses and he had already been charged. His moment of truth telling had disappeared after that first apology.

I was disappointed in his choice to move from integrity to a lie.

Swiss Chard

TWO WAYS

Swish chard is one of my favourite veggies—it is really good with most mains and it is full of vitamins. We grow it almost year-round on Pender Island. It's great served steamed (the first way) or sautéed (the second way). You can swap in kale for the chard for either of these.

FIRST WAY

Finely chop the chard, steam it lightly, and serve with a little butter, scant salt and lots of good pepper.

SECOND WAY

Sauté your chard with a little garlic and onion. Finish with some red pepper flakes or a pinch of cayenne.

Asian Broccoli

Try this with chicken thighs.

Several stalks of broccoli, cut into florets

1 jar of VH Medium Garlic Marinade

Cornstarch

Garlic, crushed

Knob of ginger, grated

2 tbsp sugar or honey

Hot sauce or chili peppers

Cashews or peanuts, crushed

Green onion, chopped

Mix all of the ingredients except the broccoli, nuts and green onion and cook till slightly thick. Steam and drain your broccoli, then pour the sauce overtop. Top with nuts and green onion.

★ **Another very simple way to prepare steamed broccoli is to add some melted butter and lemon juice. Then just finish with salt and pepper!**

Cauliflower

THREE WAYS

Cauliflower is wonderful roasted (the first way) or steamed (the second way). The third way is based on an interesting side dish we tried once during a trip to Seattle.

★ **Try orange cauliflower. I love it with lemon and butter!**

FIRST WAY

1 head cauliflower

Vegetable oil

Cumin

Curry powder

Turmeric

Cayenne (optional)

Slice the cauliflower like a steak and grill in oil. Sprinkle with cumin, curry powder, turmeric and cayenne. Finish in the oven until tender and garnish with fresh mint, cilantro or chopped parsley.

SECOND WAY

1 head cauliflower

Butter

Lemon

Steam the cauliflower until tender, then cover it with a sauce made from melted butter and lemon. It's also delicious with a cheese sauce, which is just a white sauce with the cheese of your choice melted into it. Tried and true!

THIRD WAY

1 head cauliflower

Paprika oil

Currants

Lemon juice

Fennel pollen

Soak a head of cauliflower overnight in paprika oil (I make my own). Sauté the cauliflower, sprinkle with currants and finish with a splash of lemon juice and some fennel pollen.

Growing Asparagus

I REMEMBER MANY SPRING phone calls from my parents: "Drop by on your way home from work. We have extra asparagus for you!" I'd arrive at the home I grew up in and Mom would hand me an *au gratin* dish of fully prepared asparagus, garnished with wedges of fresh lemon.

One day, driving up Victoria Hill in Edmonton, I see people picking something on the south-facing hill. I'm told they are picking asparagus. It had probably been planted years ago, when the area was farmland or in large gardens that had since gone wild and spread to the hillside.

Asparagus is very easy to grow and, once established, is a sturdy perennial that appears in early spring. It can be harvested for about six to eight weeks in May and June. After harvest, the stalks go to seed, becoming a lovely, feathery fern-like plant. Asparagus grown at the back of a flower garden makes a lovely backdrop. Today in our yard on Pender Island, we have ninety asparagus plants, and I would happily have more!

Family Asparagus

Until you have tasted fresh organic asparagus from the garden, you have not had real asparagus.

Asparagus, broken at the base, fresh from the garden

Butter

Fresh lemon juice

Salt and pepper

Stand the stalks upright in a steaming basket, base-down, and steam until just al dente. Serve with butter, fresh lemon juice, salt and pepper.

Don's Yummy Spuds

This recipe uses ruckles, which are produced by Salt Spring Island Cheese Company. A ruckle is a soft, fresh goat milk cheese log marinated in grapeseed oil with herbs and fresh garlic.

A bunch of red-skinned potatoes, skin scrubbed and left on

Blob of butter

Kosher salt

A few splashes of buttermilk

Fresh chives, chopped

About 4 ruckles, oil and all

Cook potatoes in a large pot and gently smash them. Toss with remaining ingredients while still warm.

★ Use your favourite soft cheese if you can't find any ruckles.

Baby Potatoes

TWO WAYS

There is nothing nicer than new veggies fresh from the garden, and baby potatoes are at the top of my list!

★ All ovens cook differently, so the temperatures won't always be exact. Get to know yours and work with it.

FIRST WAY

Baby potatoes

Oil

Garlic, minced

Fresh rosemary

Grainy mustard

Shallots, minced

Toss washed spuds with remaining ingredients. Roast at 425 degrees for 1 hour.

SECOND WAY

Baby potatoes

Fresh parsley

Chives

Butter

Cook potatoes in water with a little salt. Drain and add parsley, chives and a good smash of butter.

Re-stuffed Potatoes

This is one of the easiest, greatest things to do with potatoes. These spuds can be done ahead. I have even frozen them.

Several large baking potatoes

Sour cream

Buttermilk

Green onions, chopped

Butter

Egg

Bacon bits (homemade is best)

Cheddar cheese, grated

Paprika

Bake the potatoes and let them cool. Once cooled, scoop the insides out and place in a bowl with sour cream, buttermilk, green onions, butter, egg and bacon. Mix until the lumps are gone.

Stuff the filling back in the shells and top with a little cheddar cheese and paprika. Re-bake until crisp on top and warm through.

Gentle Mashed Potatoes

A mild, cheesy and creamy way to serve potatoes.

Garden-fresh potatoes, peeled

Butter, melted

Milk, buttermilk or cream, warmed

Pinch of salt

About half a package of Boursin Garlic & Fine Herbs cheese (or similar)

Boil potatoes till cooked, then drain, dry and mash. In a separate pot, combine the remaining ingredients. Use your judgement on amounts, depending on how moist you want your potatoes.

Combine the mixture with the potatoes and transfer into a casserole dish to serve immediately, or refrigerate until ready to reheat.

Creamed Potato Casserole

This is a good, hearty, crowd-pleasing winter dish.

6 or 7 Yukon Gold or Russet potatoes

1 cup cream

3 cloves garlic, whole

½ cup grated cheese (fontina or gruyere)

Salt and pepper

Slice the potatoes. Warm the cream on the stovetop with the garlic cloves. When warm, discard garlic. Layer the potatoes, cheese and cream in a casserole dish, finishing with cheese. Bake for 45 minutes at 350 degrees. Season with salt and pepper to taste.

Mom's Potato Pancakes

On many chilly winter nights when I was a child, we had these pancakes with stew or a pot roast. I still use this recipe. Sometimes I add some grated onion and chives. After grating the potatoes, be sure they are very dry.

★ **Don't worry if the potatoes change colour before they are cooked. Once they are heated, they will become white again.**

2 cups raw potato, grated

2 tbsp onion, minced

2 eggs, slightly beaten

2 tbsp flour

1 tsp baking powder

Pinch of salt

Mix all ingredients except potatoes, adding them last. Drop the mixture by spoonfuls on a heated, greased griddle. Cook until golden brown, turning only once. They can be cooked ahead and reheated. They also freeze well.

Potatoes, Potatoes, Potatoes

I LOVE ALL TYPES OF POTATOES. I prefer organic, and nothing beats spuds fresh from the garden. But growing potatoes in BC is difficult, because they often become infested with wireworms.

The first couple of years we plant potatoes we are lucky to have no pest problems. One day, Don asks Mikah to go up to the garden with him to get a few potatoes for supper. Eagerly, Mikah goes along. Upon arriving in the potato patch, Mikah says, "But there are no potatoes here."

"Ah, but we dig for them, Mikah," Don says.

This is like asking Mikah to seek out a hidden treasure, and getting him to stop digging proves difficult.

Years later, we can no longer get pest-free potatoes, but still want to grow them. So, we decide to experiment. We plant our potatoes in a raised bed, then cover the bed with some reemay cloth (also known as row cover) that we buy at Lee Valley Tools. We have perfect spuds again! Now, our three-year-old grandson Henry gets to experience the same excitement Mikah did, harvesting potatoes as they magically appear from the ground.

Noni's Spinach Pie

Long ago, I developed this pie to serve with lamb dinners. Sometimes I serve it on other occasions, but it really works best with lamb. I often make three or four at a time and freeze them.

★ **To save the chopping, swap a handful of dried onion for the fresh onion.**

Filo pastry

Butter, melted

5 boxes of frozen spinach, drained (or fresh, using about the same amount)

3 eggs, beaten

About ¼ cup of fresh dill

1 cup cottage cheese, run through the food processor

1 cup crumbled feta cheese

Salt and pepper

1 small sweet onion, chopped

Thaw the pastry and follow the directions on the box to prevent it drying out. Melt the butter and have it ready with a pastry brush.

Mix all the filling ingredients in a large bowl. Place the filling in baking pans and top with filo. Do not put a bottom crust on it—it truly is better without it.

Apply the pastry one sheet at a time, buttering each sheet as you go. Don't worry if it breaks, because it probably will—that only adds to the character. I put about 7 or 8 layers of filo on each pie.

When assembled, freeze the pies or cook them at about 375 degrees to start, then lower the heat until they are cooked—use your judgement. It is easy and you really can't wreck these pies.

Mushroom Party Tart

I serve this tart as an accompaniment when I am doing a buffet dinner with roast beef, salads and breads. Mushroom lovers love this!

★ **Cookware counts in all recipes. Always use the best you can afford!**

1 thin-crust pizza base, baked (see page 94)

A large bunch of mixed mushrooms (your choice)

1 large onion, chopped

Several cloves garlic, chopped

1 bunch parsley or cilantro, or a mix

A dash of chili powder

A splash of dry white wine or vermouth

1 package of pepper goat cheese

6 oz cream cheese

Sauté mushrooms, garlic and onions, then add parsley or cilantro and chili powder. Finish cooking with a splash of white wine.

Mix the cheeses and spread on the thin-crust pizza. Top with the cooled mushroom mixture.

I usually prepare the tart to this stage and refrigerate it for a day. Heat it at 350 degrees until warmed through, then serve.

Marvellous Mushrooms

These mushrooms are really good, and they can be prepared ahead. I make them to accompany steak or roast beef.

A large assortment of mushrooms, washed and chopped

Good-quality olive oil and butter

2 cloves fresh garlic, finely chopped

1 large sweet onion, chopped

Parsley, chopped

Madeira or sherry

Worcestershire sauce

Dollop of beef demi-glaze

Add butter and oil to a heavy frying pan, then add garlic, onions and mushrooms. Sauté until almost cooked, then add parsley, a couple of shots of Worcestershire sauce, about ¼ cup of Madeira and a dollop of a good demi-glaze. Cook slowly until all the flavours have meshed, then cool and refrigerate until ready to use.

★ **Don't skip the Madeira—that is what adds the volume of flavour.**

Mashes

I love veggie mashes. You can mash just about anything and freeze it until you need it. I use my food processor to mash, and in the case of Brussels sprouts, I process only until the chopped stage. Here are a few of my favourite mashes.

Broccoli Butter and lemon go so well with broccoli that I seldom do my broccoli any other way. I sometimes top it with chopped toasted nuts (almonds, hazelnuts, pecans or walnuts). If you want something different, all cheeses go well with broccoli. So does a combination of anchovies, lemon, black olives (pitted and chopped) and capers—combine these into a sauce and mix into the mash.

Brussels Sprouts Fine chopping totally changes these vicious little veggies most people love to hate. When I first had Brussels sprouts in a mash served with a lamb curry, I had no idea what I was eating. All I knew was that I loved it! My favourite way to dress them is with butter, sugar and really good balsamic vinegar, finished with salt and pepper. For variety, you could go the curry, cumin and apple route with pecans or walnuts and, of course, sugar.

Carrots These are good either mashed alone or in combo with parsnips or squash. Add a little butter and salt. If you want other flavours, chicken stock, dill, sugar, lemon, orange juice, ginger, curry and cumin go well with carrots. Occasionally I add a beaten egg to bind my mash.

Cauliflower It makes a lovely mash. My choices of additions would be butter, cream, a beaten egg, salt and cheese (just about any kind or a combination of cheeses will work beautifully). I tend to keep this mash mild.

Kohlrabi I love kohlrabi! You can combine it with carrots, turnips and rutabaga, a little sugar, butter, salt and pepper. Sometimes I do a carrot, kohlrabi and parsnip mash.

Turnips I like turnips with apple and a little sugar. Tossing in a few carrots would be fine.

Winter Squashes I dress this mash in a similar way to the carrot mash. Apple is always a nice addition to squash. Of course, you will season your mash to partner with the rest of the meal.

Yams and Sweet Potatoes I usually buy a combination of varieties of yams and sweet potatoes when they are in season and mix them all with a little butter, salt and pepper.

Tomato Tart

**This tart is so easy and really good.
I serve it as a side dish.**

8 sheets of filo pastry

Butter, melted

Cheese (goat or any other cheese you like)

Cherry tomatoes, cut in half

Garlic cloves, roasted

Pitted olives (optional)

Marinated artichoke hearts, sliced

Basil, chopped

Parsley, chopped

Grate or process the cheese through a food processor and set aside. Layer the filo pastry in a rectangular pan, buttering between layers. Place a layer of the cheese mixture on the filo. Next, top with lots of cherry tomatoes cut in half, with the cut side up. Tuck in some roasted garlic cloves, olives and the artichokes. Sprinkle with the basil and parsley, then bake at 350 degrees until brown around the edges.

When you are ready to serve, top with thinly sliced tomatoes and more fresh basil.

Dad's Tomato Casserole

A favourite from my childhood.

1 onion, chopped

½ red pepper, diced

1 to 1½ cups cremini mushrooms, sliced

½ cup fontina cheese

2 cans organic unsalted tomatoes, chopped

4 slices buttered toast, cubed

4 tbsp dry sherry

1 tbsp lemon juice

1½ tsp sugar

2 tbsp oregano

Parmesan, grated

Sauté onion, mushrooms, and red peppers in oil, but don't brown. Drain and add to remaining ingredients. Top with Parmesan and bake at 350 degrees for 30 minutes.

Stuffed Tomatoes

A delicious side dish or light main!

★ My children learned to cook and garden at an early age. You don't need to live on a farm to grow tomatoes—this can be done in the city!

4 large ripe tomatoes

½ cup bread crumbs, toasted

Artichoke hearts, chopped

Fresh parsley and basil, finely chopped

A few shakes of garlic powder

Grated cheese of your choice

Chop off the stem end of the tomatoes, scoop out the seeds and fill the tomatoes with the mixture. Top with grated cheese and bake at 350 degrees until tender.

A Festive Dinner

THANKSGIVING IS ONE OF my favourite festive events, and autumn on the Prairies is truly wonderful. This year we are in Calgary. I love the sunny days walking along the shores of the Bow River. Leaves changing colours and fallen leaves crunching under my feet. The Bow, tumbling and rushing along over river rocks in all shapes and shades of grey, is a cobalt blue, reflecting the clear azure sky—these sights for me capture the essence of a warm autumn Prairie afternoon. The fragrance of warm, dried leaves and high bush cranberries… what could be better?

Back home after our walk with Misha, it's time to get ready for Thanksgiving dinner. This year, I have decided to use all my good china and silver. As I hold a large silver fork, I wonder: how many Thanksgivings has this fork attended? How many turkeys have been served with this fork? Beautifully ornate, it is an antique from my father's grandmother. I am told she was a wise and wily Irish woman, though mostly my heritage is Scottish.

As I set the table with silver and handmade Italian plates, I wonder why I don't use this elegant tableware more often. The answer is simple: it's easier not to. We live in busy times. Dishwasher-safe utensils can look nice and are very practical, but nostalgia can be wonderful too.

Squash

TWO WAYS

The first way (steaming) is best for a winter squash. Use a nice butternut squash for the second, roasted way.

FIRST WAY

1 squash, cubed

Butter

Brown sugar

Sage (optional)

Cut squash into chunks and steam. Finish with a little butter and brown sugar, and sprinkle with sage.

SECOND WAY

1 squash, cubed

2 pears, cored and peeled

Butter, melted

Salt and pepper

Brown sugar

Allspice (optional)

Chicken stock (low sodium)

Pour melted butter into a baking dish. Place squash and pears in the pan. Sprinkle with salt and pepper, a couple of spoonfuls of brown sugar and a pinch of allspice. Pour chicken stock over the mixture. Bake at 350 degrees for about 1 hour or until tender.

Curried Fruit

I like to serve this fruit mixture with ham.

★ **Any combination of dried, fresh or canned fruit will work for this recipe.**

1 can pears, in juice

1 can peaches, in juice

1 can pineapple, in juice

1 can pitted cherries

3 fresh mangos

A splash of Triple Sec

½ cup dried cranberries

⅓ cup melted butter

½ cup brown sugar (or less)

5 to 6 tbsp curry powder

Drain the fruit, then assemble in a casserole dish and splash with Triple Sec. Combine remaining ingredients and pour overtop. Bake uncovered at 325 degrees till warm. Do not overcook.

Desserts

Almond Cake

This is a simple cake to serve with fruit.

⅔ cup butter

1 cup sugar

1 tbsp almond extract

4 eggs

½ cup milk

1 tbsp vanilla

1½ cup toasted almond flour

1 cup flour

2 tsp baking powder

Mix all ingredients together. Bake at 350 degrees until a knife inserted in the centre comes out clean.

Yummy Loaf

I have made many, many of these loaves and I highly recommend them.

1 cup butter

1 cup sugar

3 eggs

1 tbsp hot water

1 tsp lemon juice

1 tbsp lemon rind

2 cups flour

½ tsp baking powder

½ tsp salt

1½ cup currants

¾ cup toasted pecans

GLAZE

2 tbsp corn syrup

Lemon juice

Combine ingredients. Bake at 275 degrees for about 1¾ hours or less, until done. After removing it from the oven, spread 2 tbsp of corn syrup and a dash of lemon juice over the warm loaf.

Fun Kids' Birthday Cake

When my children were little, we made a quick and easy cake together every year for their parties. The guests loved it and it was easy to eat—no crumbs or mess anywhere! Each year we created it in a different shape, such as Mickey Mouse, a teddy bear, a rabbit or a clown. Really, you can do anything—the mixture is so easy to work with. Decorating is marvellous; let your imagination run wild. Use candies of every shape and colour, and follow the lead of your little helper. Adjust the ingredients to suit your needs. Have fun!

★ I really believe that if you bring kids to a table with ingredients or other materials, give them some direction, keep them safe and watch them go, amazing, creative masterpieces result!

6 Mackintosh's toffee bars

About 6 tbsp cream or homogenized milk

7½ cups Rice Krispies

Place the Rice Krispies in a large, greased bowl. Smash the toffee while it is still in its box. Melt the toffee with the milk or cream in a double boiler or a very heavy-bottomed pot. (Adjust the amount of cream or milk as needed to get a workable consistency.)

When the mixture is blended, pour it over the Rice Krispies. Mix, and while still warm, mould into desired shape. Now play!

The March of the Baked Alaska

WE ARE HAVING LUNCH at a fun little bistro in Calgary. Suzanne, my daughter, suggests dessert. "Sure, why not?" I reply. We select a choco terrine with peanut meringue.

The dessert arrives, and for Suzanne, it is new and unique. For me, it brings memories flooding back of my parents and the baked Alaska we enjoyed so long ago at the "Hotel Mac."

The Hotel MacDonald in Edmonton, now a Fairmont hotel, sits on the edge of downtown, regally overlooking the North Saskatchewan River. The restaurant at the hotel used to hold a regular event called the March of the Baked Alaska: on every large special occasion, the entire serving staff would march into the massive dining room carrying the baked Alaskas adorned with sparklers. The desserts were taken to the head table, then cut and distributed. As I recall, the waiters were piped in by bagpipes.

The dessert Suzanne and I share is not a baked Alaska, but it has a similar meringue topping. It is delicious all the same, and we enjoy it with two wonderful cappuccinos.

Baked Alaska

Serve this topped with raspberry coulis or other sauce of your liking.

★ **Any kind of sponge cake and any kind of ice cream will work!**

Sponge cake

Ice cream

8 egg whites, beaten

Pinch of cream of tartar

1 cup sugar

Top the sponge cake with ice cream and place in the freezer. Let it set.

Beat the egg whites, sugar and tartar powder until stiff, then spread completely over the cake and ice cream so it is sealed. Return to freezer for 1 hour. Remove from the freezer and bake at 425 degrees for 8 to 10 minutes. Serve immediately.

Molten Chocolate Cakes

These are so easy, but so good. I sometimes dish the mixture into the ramekins ahead of time, then pop them in the oven as supper is starting.

½ cup butter

8 oz of the best dark chocolate you can get

4 to 5 eggs

1½ to 2 tsp vanilla extract

½ cup sugar

2 tbsp flour

Melt the butter and chocolate. Beat together the eggs, vanilla, sugar and flour and fold this mixture into the butter and chocolate. This can be made ahead and refrigerated until needed.

Grease some single-serving ramekins with butter and fill. Bake at 400 degrees for about 10 to 12 minutes, or until the cakes are slightly jiggly in the centre.

★ **These are wonderful served with a bowl of crème fraiche.**

Strawberry Shortcake

This one is a keeper!

Sponge cake or white cake

Mascarpone

Sugar to taste

Whipping cream

Strawberries, mashed, reserving some juice

1 package Knox gelatin

TOPPING

Fresh strawberries

Mint leaves

Place a metal expandable mould (about 4 inches high) on a plate and coat with nonstick spray. Cut the cake to fit the mould and place in the bottom (it should come about halfway up the sides).

In the food processor, combine the mascarpone, sugar and cream. Blend and add strawberries.

If you have some strawberry juice from the mashed berries or water, mix with the Knox gelatin. Soften in the microwave and add to the strawberry/cream mixture. Pour on top of the cake and smooth it out.

Refrigerate or freeze. Garnish with fresh strawberries and mint leaves.

Fruit Cake

Fruit cake is a must for us at Christmas and a delight throughout the year. For mine, I use dried pears, yellow raisins, apricots, dried mango, cherries (both dry and maraschino), orange rind and lemon rind.

3 cups flour

½ tsp baking powder

⅔ cup almond flour

1½ cups butter

1 cup sugar

Vanilla

Almond extract

4 eggs

Lots of rum

Fruit of your choice

Line tins with parchment paper, sprayed or buttered. Combine all ingredients and add to tins. Cook in a very low-temperature oven until done.

Lemon Party Cake

This summer cake looks wonderful—it is a showstopper and so easy. I recently served it after a lamb curry and it really worked. As usual, all amounts and ingredients are approximate.

1 sponge cake, cut into layers

½ tbsp Knox gelatin

About 2 tbsp icing sugar

1 tub mascarpone

About 1 cup of whipping cream, whipped

Lemon curd

Liqueurs of your choice (I like Triple Sec)

Lots of wonderful fresh fruit, preferably organic

Dissolve the gelatin in cold water, then heat in the microwave. Combine the mascarpone, icing sugar and whipped cream. Add the gelatin and let cool.

Put the cream mixture between the cake layers. Place a cuff of parchment paper, cut to fit and taped, around the cake to keep everything evenly stacked. (Have the cuff come up about 3 inches above the top of the cake.) Carefully spread the lemon curd on the top of the cake and refrigerate. Set the fresh fruit to soak in the liqueur.

A few hours before serving, stack the top of the cake with the soaked fruit. Add a light gelatin mixture to give it stability and shine. Remove parchment cuff just before serving.

Cupcakes

"**HI, MOM! DO YOU** want to come to the cupcake shop with me?" asks my daughter Lisa. "Sure!" I answer. Lisa, like me, is a foodie. If she is driving across town for cupcakes, there must be a good reason.

I am curious. A cupcake shop? The little shop is charming, with a cheery exterior that provides a wonderful welcome. Inside, movement is almost impossible. It is jam-packed with customers, all waiting for their turn to purchase cupcakes.

Behind an old-fashioned glass display case, cupcakes of all varieties proudly sit on their silver pedestals, waiting to be packed into containers. They have names like Sweet Memory, Love Flow, Blue Magic, Lemon Sweet, Cosmo, Sweet Lava, Chocolate Princess and Carrot Cream.

"Is this an American chain?" I ask Lisa. "No, I think it's local," she answers. Now I am really curious. This little operation is so slick and seems to have found a niche market. Something that represents home, warmth, safety and good memories.

A few days later, I visit the shop again on my own. I purchase a Chocolate Princess cupcake and take it with a latte to the sandy beach at English Bay. As I sit on a log with my treat, watching the sailboats leisurely amble out to sea, the wind gently blows over the sparkling marine blue waters. I feel incredible peace. I munch my cupcake, through the fluffy, light-pink buttercream icing covered with shiny sprinkles, and into the rich, moist chocolate. Yes, this is definitely comfort food.

I search my memory for a time when cupcakes were part of my life. I realize that when I was around five years old, one of the best parties I attended served cupcakes. I recall the happy time, the friendship and family. The warm, happy feelings linger inside me.

Cupcakes can fill a void and help you feel safe, innocent, almost childlike. They can offer a reprieve from some of the unpleasant events of today's world.

This new cupcake shop is helping us all get in touch with our good memories.

My Cupcakes

I have a formula I have used for two weddings, for each of which I have made nearly 100 cupcakes. They were very well received both times. They had to be made ahead and, in one case, transported to a different city. That meant freezing.

First, I use a really good cake mix, then doctor it up a bit to ensure the cake is moist. For example, with a chocolate mix, I add a bit of good-quality chocolate. I make a variety each time I do this, but use the same basic formula. Some of the flavours I use are chocolate, chai, lemon, coconut and raspberry.

For the icing, I use a combination of icing sugar, mascarpone, whipping cream and whatever flavouring and colour I want to use.

Crunchy Crisp Cookies

Yum!

1 cup butter

1 cup brown sugar

2 eggs

1½ cups rolled oats

1 cup very finely shredded coconut

1½ cups flour

¼ tsp baking soda

2 tsp baking powder

2 tsp vanilla

A few twists of freshly grated nutmeg

Mix the ingredients (adding in the order listed), roll into little balls and flatten with a fork. Bake at 350 degrees for about 10 minutes.

Chocolate Delight Squares

This is a simple, wonderful recipe.

★ **This recipe might be fun to try with a really good dark chocolate.**

16 to 20 marshmallows

¼ cup milk

2 Jersey Milk bars, broken up

1 cup whipping cream, whipped

2 cups graham cracker crumbs

1 tbsp icing sugar

½ cup butter

Gently melt the first three ingredients, then mix and cool. Add the cream to the cooled chocolate mixture and set aside.

Mix the crumbs, sugar and melted butter. Line a pan with all but 3 tbsp of the crumb mix. Pour chocolate mixture over the crumbs and top with the remaining crumbs. Chill and cut into squares.

Date Squares

These were a staple in our home while growing up, and today I make a fairly light version. These squares freeze really well.

★ **If you use lemon juice, you may need to increase the sugar.**

FILLING

About 3 cups good-quality dates, chopped

¼ cup sugar

1 cup water

½ cup fresh orange juice or 2 tbsp lemon juice

BASE AND TOP

½ cup butter

¾ cup brown sugar

1 cup flour

1 cup oats

Mix the filling ingredients in a pot and cook until thick. Set aside to cool.

Mix the base ingredients next, then spread half of the base on the bottom of a 9-inch pan. Spread the date filling over the base and top with the remaining mix. Bake at 350 degrees for about 30 minutes.

Fig Tarts

THREE WAYS

We have several fig trees on Pender Island and we enjoy their bounty very much. Fresh figs are wonderful, and fig tarts are truly amazing! I make about six at a time and freeze them.

★ **For fig tarts, use a rectangular pan with fluted edges and a removable bottom.**

FIRST WAY

Fresh figs

1 pastry base (see page 264)

Raspberry jam

Honey

Cinnamon

Almonds, toasted and chopped

CUSTARD

½ container mascarpone

¼ cup sugar

1 egg

A good splash of vanilla

Line a pan with pastry, partially cook it, then let it cool. Add a smear of raspberry jam on top of the pastry.

Mix the custard ingredients together and pour into the pastry. Arrange fresh figs, cut in half, on the custard. Carefully drizzle honey on the figs and sprinkle with cinnamon. Scatter some finely chopped toasted almonds on top. Bake at 375 degrees for about 20 minutes.

SECOND WAY

Puff pastry

Soft cheese

Chives

Fresh figs

Balsamic vinegar

Start with a base of store-bought puff pastry and follow its directions to bake. When the pastry is cooked, spread a soft cheese and chives on it and top with freshly cut figs. Drizzle with balsamic vinegar. Serve warm or at room temperature.

THIRD WAY

Filo pastry

Soft goat cheese or blue cheese

Fresh figs

Toasted walnuts

Italian parsley

Spread filo pastry with a soft goat cheese or blue cheese. Cut fresh figs in half and arrange on the pastry. Top with some toasted walnuts and bake at 350 to 375 degrees till cooked (about 10 minutes). Garnish with Italian parsley.

Easy No-Bake Peanut Butter Squares

These were a favourite when my kids were little.

½ cup butter

½ cup peanut butter (no salt or sugar added)

6 oz package butterscotch chips

2 cups miniature marshmallows

Melt butter, then add peanut butter and mix together. Add butterscotch chips and marshmallows. Press into pan and chill.

Ginger Cookies

A great Christmas treat!

½ cup butter

1 large egg

⅔ cup dark brown sugar, plus extra for rolling

¼ cup molasses

1 tbsp fresh grated ginger

2 cups flour

2 tbsp baking soda

¼ tsp allspice

Cinnamon

Nutmeg

1 egg white (for dipping)

Mix all ingredients except the egg white into balls the size of a large marble. Coat in egg white, then roll in brown sugar. Press balls down. Bake at 350 degrees for 7 to 8 minutes.

★ **Most kinds of cookie batter can be made ahead and frozen. You can even shape them first!**

Christmas Bake-a-Thon

FOR MANY YEARS my daughter Suzanne and I have held an annual bake-a-thon, as she calls it. It has become one of our Christmas traditions. We pick a day and bake all kinds of cookies and squares to be shared with family and friends over the holidays. Recipes old and new are brought out and considered. Ingredients are purchased and, with coffee in hand and aprons on, off to work we go!

One year, six-year-old Mikah declares that blue is his favourite colour. Every cookie he can get his hands on has some blue icing on it and lots of sprinkles. Flour flies all over the kitchen and every cupboard handle shines with butter.

At mid-morning, the doorbell rings and Clarissa, a friend of Suzanne's, arrives with her mother-in-law Bea. Bea is in town from Saskatoon. Now we have four generations participating in our bake-a-thon.

Soon the doorbell rings again and it's two of Suzanne's colleagues. By 5 p.m. the whole group is still here.

The warm house vibrates with laughter and tales of how it used to be—not from Bea, the eldest, but from the girls remembering their own mothers' homes at Christmas. Bea educates us all on travel, the internet, dancing and her vibrant social life. She is an amazing and positive lady in her late eighties, and a role model for all of us.

I stumble out into the chilly winter air around suppertime, filled with more joy than I can imagine, heading home with cookies and squares all tucked in their boxes to share.

Marion's Thumbprint Cookies

Suzanne and I have been doing our Christmas baking together since 2006. We make all kinds of cookies, squares, some candy and Christmas pudding. When my friend Marion heard what we were doing, she offered this simpler version of thumbprint cookies.

3 cups flour

½ cup icing sugar

1¼ cups soft butter

2 tsp vanilla

1 egg

1 cup raspberry jam

TOPPING

2 squares chocolate, melted

1 tsp butter, melted

Mix everything except the jam and toppings into a ball. Press the dough onto a cookie sheet lined with parchment paper, with a score where you want to cut the squares. Make a little hole in the centre of each square and place a dollop of jam in each hole. Bake at 350 degrees for about 15 minutes. They should be a light golden colour.

Mix the topping ingredients together and drizzle over the cookies. Cut into squares.

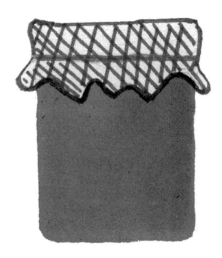

Pear Streusel

This recipe is easy, fast and fabulous! My former mother-in-law often served this on cold winter Sunday evenings.

1 large can good-quality pears
(or fresh poached pears)

½ cup flour

½ cup brown sugar

¾ cup shredded coconut

⅓ cup butter

Mix everything but the pears, and place half of the mixture in a baking dish. Arrange drained pears, cut side down, on top, then top with the remaining mixture. Bake at 425 degrees for 7 minutes, then at 350 degrees for 15 minutes longer.

Noni's Brownies

I like to try different flours for these. If you like, substitute ¼ cup almond flour for the same amount of flour.

1 cup sugar

2 squares unsweetened chocolate

2 eggs

2 tsp vanilla

½ cup butter

¾ cup flour

Mix, pour into a baking pan and bake at 350 degrees for 30 minutes.

★ **To make this brownie even tastier and chewier, add raisins that have been soaked in boiling water. Soaked sour cherries work great too!**

Mile-High Apple Pie

IT ALL BEGINS WHEN Don is on a flight from Toronto to Vancouver. He sees an article in *Pacific Yachting* magazine about low bank waterfront land for sale on a place called Pender Island. Pender is one of the Southern Gulf Islands, located between Vancouver and Victoria.

Don bursts through the door when he gets home, luggage in one hand and article in the other. "I need dirt," he says.

We phone a realtor, make an appointment and head over to see this piece of property. I feel really uncertain about this adventure, but as we glide through the Pacific waters to our destination, I can't help but be touched by the incredible beauty. The stately evergreens reach for a clear blue sky, and bold strong roots line the shores, dipping into a cold ocean. I am awestruck by the quiet, calm feeling.

We arrive at a sloping, three-and-a-half-acre lot filled with moss, long grass, wild shrubs, rock and an abundance of tall trees. As we make our way carefully down to the sea, we reach a small plateau. "This is where the house will go," Don states with clarity. I am clear about nothing.

Before we leave the property, Don has it all mapped out. Me, not so much. After all, I am city, through and through.

We stop in the island's small shopping centre for coffee and to discuss possibly buying the land with the realtor, who insists we buy an apple pie from the local bakery to take home. He purchases one every time he visits the island, he says, and he tells us they are the best ever.

Several hours later we leave Pender Island with the tallest apple pie I have ever seen, along with a piece of rugged, untamed land. The realtor is right: the mile-high apple pie truly is the best—perfectly sugared and seasoned. A couple of years later, after many ups and downs, we step into our new cottage by the sea.

Years later, I walk up our winding road from the sea and am struck by the beauty, serenity and peace in this soul-enriching place. As the sun peeks through the tall trees, the birds sing their morning songs. I move past the fragrant flowers to pick some fresh, plump, sweet blueberries for breakfast.

This is true bliss, with our dog Misha by my side.

Pumpkin Pie

Thanksgiving goes hand in hand with pumpkin pie. I always partially cook the crust before adding the filling. To keep the bottom of the crust flat, I use a metal chain device I bought from Williams-Sonoma.

1 pie shell

FILLING

16 oz Pacific organic pumpkin purée (or 1 large can)

¾ to 1 cup brown sugar

CUSTARD

⅔ cup canned evaporated milk

3 to 4 eggs

1 tsp cinnamon

1 tsp nutmeg

Pinch of ginger

Pinch of cloves

1 tbsp flour

In a saucepan, cook the pumpkin and sugar for about 5 minutes while stirring.

In a large bowl, mix together the custard ingredients. Then, mix the hot pumpkin in with the custard mixture and pour into the hot pie shell. Bake at 425 degrees for 15 minutes, then reduce to 325 to 350 degrees and bake for approximately 1 hour. Check near the end of baking to prevent overcooking.

Pull out the pie when the centre is still slightly wiggly; it will become solid as it cools.

★ **Serve with whipped cream, of course!**

Pecan or Mincemeat Tarts

Tart shells

MINCEMEAT FILLING

1 jar President's Choice mincemeat

1 jar Crosse & Blackwell mincemeat

6 to 8 apples, chopped

6 to 8 pears, chopped

Large bag of frozen cherries, chopped

Handful of golden raisins

2 cups currants

Lemon and orange zest

Nutmeg

Cinnamon

Allspice

PECAN FILLING

2 large eggs

1 tbsp heavy cream

¼ cup packed light brown sugar

1 tsp flour

1 tbsp melted butter

Splash of dark rum

½ cup corn syrup

¼ tsp of grated nutmeg

1 cup pecans, chopped

Vanilla

Freshly grated nutmeg

For mincemeat tarts, simmer ingredients in a large pot for 1 to 2 hours. Cool, then fill tart shells to ½ to ⅔ full. For pecan tarts, mix all ingredients and place in the shells up to about ⅔ full.

Bake at 350 degrees for about 20 to 25 minutes.

I love small tarts shells—they can be found in the freezer aisle at the grocery store. They are very convenient, as they can be frozen right after cooking.

★ Use good tart shells, and watch them as they bake to adjust your cooking time. You don't want to burn the bottoms.

Caramel Pots

**These are easy and fun—
do it your way!**

Caramel pudding or cheesecake filling

Chocolate wafers, crushed

Butter

TOPPING

Chocolate, melted

Salted caramel sauce

Almonds, toasted and sliced

Mix crushed chocolate wafers with a little butter and press into individual ramekins. Top with caramel pudding or cheesecake. Cover with melted chocolate, and drizzle with salted caramel sauce and toasted sliced almonds.

Coconut Cream Pots

Cute and creamy! Use individual ramekins.

8 oz Philadelphia cream cheese

⅓ container mascarpone

Vanilla

Icing sugar

Lemon rind and juice

1 can coconut milk or cream

Gelatin powder

TOPPING

Whipped cream

White chocolate

Toasted coconut

Combine all main ingredients, then fill individual ramekins and chill. When set, top as desired. Serve chilled.

Filled Choco Peanut Butter Cookies

This dessert is nice topped with Marshmallow Crème Topping (see page 251). The filling recipe can be doubled if needed.

BASE AND TOPPING

Mr. Christie's chocolate wafers
(5 per serving)

Chocolate, melted

Nuts (optional)

Marshmallow Crème Topping (optional)

FILLING

1 cup whipping cream

½ cup smooth peanut butter
(no salt or sugar)

½ cup mascarpone

¼ cup extra-fine granulated or
berry sugar (or to taste)

2 tbsp gelatin, dissolved in
a small amount of water

Whip the cream and set it aside. Mix the peanut butter, sugar and mascarpone together, then fold in the cream. Add the gelatin mixture.

Spread the mixture between the cookies and top with some melted chocolate. Put in the fridge for about 3 hours to set, then top as desired.

★ **Michelle, my friend Marion's daughter-in-law, fills glass cookie jars with wrapped treats as a gift, and adds the magic touch of placing a tiny string of battery-powered lights inside.**

Lemon Pudding

When I was a child, this was a staple in our home. My mother made it in a casserole dish and served it with cream. I prefer to cook it in individual ramekins and serve it with fresh berries in season.

4 eggs, separated

¾ cup sugar

3 tbsp melted butter

¼ cup fresh lemon juice

Rind of a lemon (to taste, depending on how tart you want it)

¼ cup flour

1½ cups milk

Separate the eggs and reserve the yolks. Stiffly beat the whites and set aside.

Combine the sugar, butter, egg yolks, lemon juice and rind. Add to flour. Add the milk and fold in the beaten egg whites. Pour the mixture into greased ramekins, then place in a larger pan containing warm water. Bake at 350 degrees until cooked (about 20 to 25 minutes).

Molten Dulce de Leche Pudding

This is an easy caramel dessert.

3 eggs

3 tbsp flour

1⅔ cup dulce de leche (can be bought in jars)

Whipped cream

Butter and flour some oven-safe ramekins. Beat the eggs for a couple of minutes, then add the dulce de leche and flour. Blend and pour into the ramekins. Bake at 400 degrees for about 12 to 14 minutes. Remove from ramekins and top with whipped cream.

Sticky Toffee Date Pudding

This is a very wonderful cold-evening pudding. Maybe something to enjoy after a long walk—it is heavy and delicious. The Upper Crust Café, a charming restaurant in Edmonton's Garneau area, sells these little puddings individually with a pecan cooked into the top and warm caramel sauce drizzled over and around them. This is my recipe, which is probably quite similar to theirs.

★ **The mixture will foam—don't panic.**

2 cups Medjool dates, pitted

2¼ cups water

1 tsp baking soda

½ cup softened butter

½ cup brown sugar

1½ tsp vanilla

3 large eggs

1¾ cup flour

1 tsp baking powder

Cook the dates in the water until soft and mushy. Remove from heat and stir in the baking soda. Cool completely.

Beat the sugar, vanilla and butter together, then add the eggs one at a time. Keep beating until light and fluffy. Blend flour and baking powder and add to the egg mixture, along with the dates. Scoop this batter into individual ramekins that have been well-buttered. Place on a cookie sheet and bake at 325 to 350 degrees for about 25 minutes. Serve warm with Basic Caramel Sauce (see page 250).

Christmas Magic

IN YEARS PAST, I EMBRACED the Christmas spirit, sharing holiday delight with friends and family.

Not this day. I reflect upon my lethargy and sadness, playing the "What If" game—and going nowhere, of course. Reality smacks me into consciousness. I begin wrapping gifts, preparing meals and finally planning to meet planes as the children come home for the holidays.

December 25 arrives. We gather, exchange gifts and stories. I participate in the merriment, burying how I really feel, or maybe just giving myself a few moments to forget what reality is. By noon, the children go to their father's house for a traditional brunch.

A hush falls over our chaotic home. Just my husband, Don, our dog Seka and me. In the quiet, vacant space there's no room for denial… tears stream down my face. I go back to the day in November when Ty, our elder Belgian shepherd, died in our arms. After many tests, surgery and misdiagnoses, our wonderful dog succumbed to cancer. A week later, during a routine checkup, Seka—a younger female Belgian shepherd—was diagnosed with terminal lung cancer and given a few weeks to live. Leaving the vet clinic that horrid day, stunned, in shock, broken-hearted and oblivious to my surroundings, I drove Seka home.

Christmas mid-day; the tree lights all mesh together through a blur of tears and waves of grief. I want to scream at God: "How can this be? It is not fair!" I am not ready to lose both my loving dogs.

Don enters the room. Gently he asks, "Do you want to take Seka to the dog park?" I would love to go to the dog park, but do I have time? A tiny voice deep inside me shouts, "Make time!" Gifted with a truly beautiful Prairie day, sunny and warm, we bundle up and pile into the car for the short ride to our dog park.

As we pull up to the curb, Seka begins howling with glee. She, like me, loves this pristine place. I wonder if she feels the positive energy I feel in our urban forest. We tumble out, running through the crunchy snow heading for "the tree"—the most special of all trees.

Hidden from the road, on a snowy secluded trail, stands a tall, majestic spruce. It is a gathering spot for dog people. At Christmastime, dozens of unique, handcrafted cards celebrating the holiday season hang from its branches. Each features the photos of one or two pets, with greetings to their two- and four-legged friends. These cards commemorate the great love that dog owners have for their pets.

"Look, Don, a card from Amos the Belgian we met a few days ago! And over here, one of our friends and their wonderful Doberman, Cariad." Included in the fifty or sixty cards fluttering in the breeze are photos of dogs since departed. Sadness wells up in me as I think of life's fragility and how fleeting our time with loved ones can be.

Seka commandingly barks, ordering us to move on. She runs ahead, tail wagging, leading us down a snowy trail to the river valley.

Trees laden with snow bend to greet us as the sun casts shadows of mysterious shapes through the branches around us. I look up to be greeted by a perfectly periwinkle blue sky. The weather and place are truly magic.

Everyone we pass stops to wish us well and we do likewise. Dogs frolic and play. One gentleman stops to show us his new camera lenses. "A Christmas indulgence," he confesses with delight, snapping photos as he walks. We have our camera too. Beautiful Seka makes a fashion statement with her green Christmas ribbon against the pure white snow.

We are like two protective parents hanging on desperately to our remaining days with our beloved dog. How can a dog that looks so healthy be gravely ill? But I saw the x-rays. I know it's real.

Again, I block the fear and sorrow, determined to enjoy the moment. Suddenly, shattering the silence, Don's cell phone rings.

"Where are you guys?" our kids ask. "We are here with Seka in the park to see the tree," I say. "We want to see the tree too!" they respond.

In the distance I see our children run, arms open. Across a white stretch of newly fallen snow, excited Seka bounds to

greet them. Together we all wander over to the tree, led by our enthusiastic dog. We take impromptu family photos and play with Seka. Don shows them the breathtaking view of our river valley.

Finally, arm in arm, we head to our vehicles to return home to finish Christmas, exchanging hellos with folks along the way. I inhale kindness and goodwill from all living things around me. I am filled with peace, comfort and joy. Like a burst of light inside me, I feel the Christmas spirit on this precious winter day.

Noni's Christmas Pudding

1½ cup flour

Pinch of salt

1 tsp baking soda

2 tsp freshly grated nutmeg

½ tsp cloves

1 tsp ginger

1 tsp cinnamon

1 cup raisins

1 cup currants

½ cup dried cherries

½ cup dried cranberries

½ cup dried apricots

Lemon rind, freshly grated

Orange rind, freshly grated

1 cup toasted pecans or walnuts

2 cups grated carrots

1 cup grated raw potato

Rum

4 eggs

1 cup brown sugar

¾ cup oil or butter

My pudding is similar to Gramma Sorence's except for one thing—I never use suet. We like this version because it is a bit healthier and still very much in keeping with the family tradition.

★ **This pudding can be modified—add ingredients that appeal to you. It also freezes well, so it can be made in advance—a great bonus at Christmastime!**

Mix the flour and spices in a bowl and set aside. In a second bowl, mix the dried fruit, rinds, nuts, carrot and potato. Pour some good-quality dark rum over this mixture and set aside.

In a third bowl, beat the eggs with the sugar and butter. Add the fruit mixture to the dry ingredients and mix, then add the wet ingredients. Mix and place in a well-greased mould.

Cover tightly and steam for about 5 hours.

Steamed Apple Pudding

I love steamed puddings served with a warm custard sauce. This is an apple version but it can be done with figs, dates or other fruits.

3 apples

½ cup butter

½ cup sugar

3 eggs

1 tsp vanilla

1 cup flour

1 tsp baking powder

1 tsp nutmeg

Dash of cinnamon

Mix apples, butter, sugar, eggs and vanilla. Mix dry ingredients, then add in the fruit mixture. Steam till cooked and a tester stuck in the centre comes out clear.

Eggnog Panna Cotta

Use a good store-bought eggnog for this.

2 cups eggnog

1 package Knox gelatin

Freshly grated nutmeg

Fresh fruit, in season

Soften gelatin in ¼ cup eggnog and dissolve in the microwave. Add to cold eggnog with nutmeg and mix well.

Divide between individual dessert dishes. Top with your favourite fruit. (I like raspberries.)

Collateral Damage

HE IS THE BEST KID EVER. He has taught me about magic with his delightfully captivating, mischievous charm, and helped me see wonder all around. When he was in our daily life, our time was filled with a joy and bliss I had never dreamed possible.

Our first grandchild, actually step-grandchild, arrives one sunny afternoon at our cottage by the sea. A bouncy five-year-old, blond, freckle-faced, jumps out of the back of the car as it comes to a halt at the end of our curving driveway, followed closely by a dog named Georgia Peach. The boy's dad and future stepmother emerge from the front seats. As eager as he is to get out of the vehicle, the child appears shy, dragging his feet along the gravel as he approaches us.

He isn't the only nervous one. I, too, feel some apprehension. This is to be a whole new experience for my husband, Don, and me. With a bit of gentle, loving encouragement from our daughter Suzanne, the child steps toward me and says, "Hi, my name is Mikah." I respond, "Hi, Mikah! It's very nice to meet you. I have heard really nice things about you. I am Noni." I don't believe in love at first sight, but this kid is pretty darn cute.

As we begin the journey of friendship, we learn many of his wonderful attributes. He is keen to learn new things and is filled with awe and adventure. Love and laughter bounce off the walls of our cottage as we discover new and fun things to do. I feel so fortunate to have this precious child in our world. Mikah loves campfires, vegetables from the garden, fishing, swimming, cooking, boating and lots of board games. In the joyful days that follow, we create many new family rituals to be enjoyed every summer, I believe, for a very long time.

Mikah really loves fishing, and I become his fishing mate. Because he is a child, he can't go to our dock by himself. He needs to go with an adult. Seeing as I am such a super fan, I am often called upon to accompany him. I usually hear, "Come on, Noni! Watch me fish." Or, "Come on, Noni! I'll teach you to fish." Off to the dock we go—him to fish and me to sit in one of the Adirondack chairs and watch. Not just casually watch, but really watch. This is serious business!

Suddenly, all hell breaks loose. He actually has a bite! A big fish on his line and it might be a salmon! Fortunately, Don is on the dock and it takes two of us to net the fish and save Mikah from being pulled into the ocean. A very delighted Mikah poses for a photo op and we take the salmon up to the house to prepare it for dinner. For dessert, we will have his favourite: chocolate fondue. Just for Mikah!

Fall and winter are spent connecting for dinner and special holidays. Early on in our relationship, I develop a special tradition. Every time they come to us for dinner, I have a small gift at Mikah's place. On one occasion, our daughter warns Mikah not to expect a gift at his place because "Noni has just arrived and won't have had time to pick anything up for you." A wise child pipes up and says, "Don't worry. There will be a gift. Guaranteed." And, of course, there is.

Hockey, winters and Alberta all go together. I have always hated hockey—really hated it. But Mikah plays, so on game days it's goodbye soft leather boots, fine wool tweeds and dress gloves, and hello heavy warm parka, ugly lined gloves, wool cap and boots so heavily lined I can barely walk. This is survival gear for a rural Alberta hockey game. Inside, the arena is cold and drafty and smells of weird food. The most challenging thing about Mikah's hockey game is getting there—often through blinding blizzards, ice, wind and cold—so, so cold! However, when the phone rings and I hear that dear little voice ask, "Hey, Noni! Are you going to come to the game?" how can I say no?

It amazes me how a little boy can light up my life and touch my soul, changing me in ways I never imagined possible.

I have a dream. I'd like to take the whole family to Hawaii. I decide the best way to do it is to rent a large house. I make it happen and off we go. The house has a pool and barbecue so days are spent eating,

swimming and surfing at the beach—all the usual things
folks do on a hot holiday. But for me, the highlight of
the trip occurs very early every morning when I hear a
tap at our bedroom door. It is Mikah. In a loud whisper
he asks if we are awake, and when we say yes, he runs
across the carpet and dives into bed between us. Once
comfortably settled, he asks if we can paint. So for about
an hour we all sit silently together, each creating works
of art—all different, but all beautiful.

I love this child more than I can put into words.

Today, I am alone at our cottage by the sea. The kid
is gone from our lives. Divorce, not death, tore him
from us. He has left now to a new stepmother and new
step-grandparents. I wonder if they are encouraged to

love and embrace him as family the way we were. We have become yesterday's grandparents.

My heart is broken, and through a blur of tears I gaze out over the ocean to our dock, once a happy place where memories linger. I look out our kitchen window to "Fort Mikah," a fort we built for him, now standing alone and empty among the tall evergreens. In the distance I hear the plaintive sound of an owl. In his room the stuffed animals stare at me with sad glassy eyes. If they could speak, they would ask for Mikah. Stillness surrounds me. Sadness hangs heavy and the whole house is haunted with an eerie quiet.

Sadly, love just wasn't enough.

Poor child. Dragged around from family to family like a piece of luggage on wheels. I wonder, is he confused and afraid? Does he feel he is to blame for the events that have unfolded? Does he feel abandoned by us? How can he know that we are also victims of this tragic event? I feel so angry and helpless. Just like Mikah, we have no voice and are banished to the past. Does he cry until all the tears are gone, alone in the dark the way I do?

Are we nothing more than collateral damage?

EPILOGUE: FINDING JEFF

FINDING JEFF IS the turning point. I no longer feel help-less and without options.

Losing Mikah left me in a very sad place, and for a long time the mention of his name brought tears to my eyes and a tightness in my chest. It felt so unfair and wrong.

A slow change begins about a year ago. While walking up South Granville I receive a text from Mikah asking if he can visit us on Pender Island.

Joy rushes through me at the possibility of Mikah re-entering our lives. I phone our daughter, who contacts Nicole, Mikah's mom. (Interestingly, both ex-wives have become close friends.) The two moms decide to book-mark the holiday for a more appropriate time, but promise Mikah it will happen.

I feel thrilled that a connection has been made.

A few days later, I hear a bing on my computer—it is an email from Mikah's dad, accusing me of things I have not done. I feel completely violated.

I need to deal with this now. For three years we all have taken emotional abuse from this self-serving man, but it stops today. Rage and helplessness turns to resolve, and I am determined to find the best, toughest custody lawyer in Calgary. I sit at the computer in Vancouver and make a list of top law firms dealing with custody issues, then phone each and every one and ask if they are the best. One firm recommends Jeff, who helps me make things right. I feel safe—finally, we have strong, intelligent man with high integrity who knows the system. No one walks over Jeff.

Now it is summer 2017, and one of the most magical holidays occurs.

In the distance I see our boat headed into the dock. I walk down from the house to greet them, three years of pain and sadness evaporating, being replaced with hope and joy.

Mikah is returning to Pender, this time with his mom Nicole, who is truly a beautiful, wise woman. Don pulls the boat into the dock and a second later a good-looking thirteen-year-old boy with reddish-blond hair and braces on his teeth swings over the side with a fishing rod in hand. He hugs me with his free arm and points his rod to the water saying, "See, Mom, this is where I caught the first and only salmon ever caught on this dock." A Coho!

There are hugs and laughter all around as this, our family, reunites. What an odd bunch we are: Don and me; Suzanne, our daughter, and her son Henry; Mikah (Henry's half-brother and Suzanne's ex-stepson). Nicole is ex-wife #1, and Suzanne is ex-wife #2. But it really works.

I feel bliss, and my hope is that everyone will have a really good few days. And we do.

Don and Mikah go fishing, bringing home a cod and a salmon. Suzanne makes amazing fish tacos for dinner, followed by Mikah's favourite, chocolate fondue.

After dinner we all sit around the fire, playing Apples to Apples. Mikah still loves games and encourages after-dinner activities.

As the stars twinkle in the black sky, I hear our laughter and see it bounce across the dark navy sea toward the distant mountains.

This is grace.

Chocolate Fondue

This is our dear Mikah's favourite dessert when he visits Pender. I like to serve everyone their own little fondue pot of chocolate with a small candle and holder underneath—these are readily available in kitchen stores and are not that expensive. The individual pots eliminate cross-contamination and dripping chocolate all over the table. Gosh, maybe I did learn something in nursing—I sure seem to know a lot about germs!

★ **Individual, self-heating fondue pots can also be used for serving drawn butter with crab and lobster.**

Good-quality, organic dark chocolate

Whipping cream

Liqueur of your choice

Fresh fruit, in season

Biscuits

Warm the chocolate in a heavy-bottomed pot with a little whipping cream and a good liqueur. When ready to serve dessert, transfer the chocolate to individual small fondue pots.

Give each guest their own pot and fondue fork, and place a large platter of fruit and biscuits on the table so people can take what they like.

Noni's Lemon Pavlova

This is my all-time favourite dessert! People tend to love it after a heavy meal. I have been making it for years; the only thing that changes is the fruit I use to accompany it. A real plus is that this can be made a day ahead. It is actually better after sitting in the fridge for a day.

★ I always mix a little softened gelatin in with my whipped cream so it stays set—kind of like spraying your hair so it holds.

6 egg whites

¼ tsp salt

¼ tsp cream of tartar

¾ cup sugar

TOPPING

Lemon curd

Whipped cream

Fresh raspberries (or your choice of fruit)

Beat egg whites until foamy, then add salt, tartar and sugar. Beat until stiff. Spread mixture on a very well-buttered pan or large pie plate. Place pavlova in a 450-degree oven, turn it off and leave the door shut for 5 hours. Don't open the door during that time. (Alternatively, when you place the pavlova in the oven, turn the oven down to 250 degrees and watch until cooked. I use this method now.)

Remove pavlova from the oven and spread with a layer of lemon curd, then top with whipped cream. Top with fresh berries or fruit.

Odds and Sods

Pender Island Ginger/Blackberry Drink

We often take a large jug of this up to the garden on hot summer days.

Ginger syrup

Blackberry sauce

Fresh blackberries

Mint, finely muddled

Lemon soda

Mint leaves

In a large container with a lid, place syrup, blackberry sauce, berries and muddled mint. Top with a large amount of lemon soda, shake and serve over ice with fresh mint leaves.

Ginger Drink

This is one of the healthiest and most refreshing drinks I have ever had. We first had it at the spa in our Hawaiian hotel. This is my version of that wonderful drink.

About 2 inches of fresh ginger, peeled and sliced

2 tbsp liquid honey (optional)

Juice of ½ lemon

Mint leaves

Bring about 2 litres of water to a boil. Add all of the ingredients and simmer for about 1 hour, then let it rest, covered, for another hour or 2. Put the drink in the fridge to chill.

★ **Serve this with a wedge of lemon or lime and a few mint leaves.**

Hockey Night on the Prairie

CRISP, COLD WINTER AIR surrounds us as we skate under the light of a solitary bulb hung in the old maple tree in our backyard. After supper, all through my childhood, every spare moment is spent on the rink during winter. It is my favourite place, no matter how cold the Prairie winter gets. I love to skate.

On school nights I am hauled in all frosty and rosy-cheeked at about 7:30 p.m. to be warmed with hot chocolate and a story. My socks and mittens hang by the fire to dry for another day of fun.

As I drift off to sleep under wool blankets and a comforter, I hear the neighbourhood boys. They have descended on the rink like a pack of hungry wolves. Now that the little kids have gone to bed, it's hockey time! Hollers and shouts mingle with the sound of the puck slamming into the fence.

Many years ago, my dad created our rink. He flooded the back garden area, removed the snow, set up lighting and maintained the rink all season. Every year of my youth, neighbourhood children were welcome—even the older boys we didn't know. The light was never turned out until hockey night on the Prairie was over.

Festive Rum

Lisa asked me to include this recipe, which was a hit with her friends when it rained at an outdoor summer event. The goal here is to fill a thermos, so depending on how strong you like it, add the rum and water accordingly.

Dark rum, good quality

Butter, a large spoonful

Nutmeg, freshly ground to taste

Zest of an orange

Hot water

A fresh cinnamon stick or two

Pour the rum into a good thermos. Add a dollop of butter and a few grates of fresh nutmeg and orange zest, then top with boiling water. Toss in one or two cinnamon sticks, seal and shake. Share with friends!

Rhu Gin Cocktail

A delicious early summer drink.

Rhubarb syrup

Long pepper syrup (just heat long peppers in a simple syrup)

Gin

San Pellegrino sparkling water

Mix syrups and gin to taste and top with San Pellegrino. Serve over chopped ice with lemon balm.

Cherry Sauce

We often put this delicious sauce on our morning cereal, but you can serve it over anything.

2 cups cherries, pitted

2 tbsp butter

¼ cup dark brown sugar

Vanilla, to taste

A tad of pure almond flavouring

Combine ingredients. Cook cherries for 5 minutes or until they start to release their juice. Serve over French toast, or use as a tart filling.

Blueberry Sauce

This sauce is good with waffles. I just pull blueberries out of the freezer to make it—they thaw in minutes.

2 cups blueberries

¼ cup sugar

1 tbsp cornstarch

Juice and rind of half a lemon

Combine the cornstarch, sugar, lemon juice and ¼ cup blueberries. Heat until the cornstarch is cooked. Turn off the heat and add the remaining berries. Add a little juice or water if needed.

★ **This recipe can be used to make a sauce out of almost any fruit.**

Orange Cream Sauce

This sauce from my daughter Suzanne is out of this world. It's delicious with vanilla gelato, gingerbread cake, poached or canned pears—or all three together!

⅔ cup butter

1¼ cup brown sugar

¾ cup heavy cream

2 tbsp orange juice concentrate

Combine and simmer for 25 minutes. Cool and store in the fridge. Serve warm.

Basic Caramel Sauce

A lovely topping for ice cream or warm cakes.

2 cups brown sugar

1 cup cream

1 cup unsalted butter

Place in heavy-bottomed pot and boil until thick. Cool slightly, then pour into a glass sealer jar and store it in the fridge—it will keep for quite a while.

★ **Remember to have the sealer jar really clean and hot or it could break.**

Maple Butter

This stuff is so good! Make it ahead and keep it in the fridge until you need it, or freeze it. It is great with waffles, pancakes and corn muffins.

1 cup butter

⅓ cup maple syrup (I use a Number 3 organic; it has the strongest flavour)

A drop of maple flavouring, if you wish

Mix and enjoy. If frozen, warm to room temperature to serve.

Marshmallow Crème Topping

Another yum!

★ **This will store for about ten days in the fridge.**

1 cup white sugar

⅔ cup light corn syrup

⅓ cup water

3 egg whites, at room temperature

¼ tsp cream of tartar

Vanilla

Heat sugar, corn syrup and water to 240 degrees. Beat eggs and tartar to soft peaks. Slowly drizzle the hot liquid into the egg whites until combined. Whip till stiff and glossy (about 8 minutes). Add vanilla.

Ain't Life Grand?

CAN THIS REALLY HAPPEN? Yes, it is happening. Love at the age of ninety-six. I am sharing this story about Edna Horner because she was a passionate gardener and cook—many of her recipes are in this book, in fact. I use the past tense because she no longer cooks or gardens; she is in a new phase of her life in an assisted living facility.

She and my grandmother were both into canning in a very big way. Today, I use Mrs. H's large canner to preserve some of our bounty from our Pender Island garden.

Life seems to be a cycle, and while Mrs. H is past her gardening, canning and cooking phase, she is busy being half of the "it couple" at her extended care home. This facility is a very lovely place with a great dining room, recreation facility and pool, a view of the mountains and lovely fireplaces. Each resident has their own small suite. In the beginning Mrs. H wasn't sure about the whole move, and, let's face it: who doesn't find change scary? Mrs. H had been a widow for nearly twenty years, enduring a loneliness that most of us can only imagine.

After Mr. Horner died, Mrs. H moved to Calgary, leaving her home and garden in the small village behind. She wanted to be closer to family. But her children worked and had children of their own in their busy city lives. When the move to assisted living first happened, it seemed like another grim step toward death. Until Lorne appeared, that is.

Lorne is ninety-three and mostly blind. Mrs. H is healthy physically but has a few memory issues. It was love at first sight! They are now inseparable. When her children come to visit she is sometimes unavailable. If you were to peek into the lush garden surrounding the care facility today you would see Lorne and Mrs. H strolling along, hand in hand, totally happy. A picture of hope and grace.

Freezer Strawberry Jam

TWO WAYS

Not long ago, we had breakfast at the Four Seasons Hotel in Vancouver. We finished off with scones and strawberry jam, the best I've ever had. Upon inquiring, I was informed it was done "in-house" and the recipe was a secret. Since that morning, I have been working on creating something similar—the first way is my closest attempt to the real thing.

The evolution of the second way began nearly forty years ago, when my dear Aunt Annie gave me a cookbook published by the Canadian Home Economics Association (she was a member). These ladies used the sun to evaporate the water in the fruit—they called it Sunshine Jam.

★ **Always use fresh local strawberries—not the mass-farmed ones that are red on the outside and white inside. You could also try the second way with different fruits, like peaches.**

FIRST WAY

Fresh strawberries, cut into pieces

½ to ¾ cup sugar

Regular Certo

Take 3 to 4 cups of cut strawberries and mix them with the sugar. Leave the mixture in the fridge overnight.

The next day, place the mixture in a large, buttered, non-reactive pan (such as an Emile Henry). It will be very watery. Cook in the oven at about 250 to 300 degrees, stirring every 15 minutes. It will take a good hour for the mixture to thicken, but it will leave you with an intense strawberry flavour. Remove and let cool.

Prepare the Certo, following the box instructions exactly for strawberry jam. Using a large clean bowl, combine your Certo and your new thick mixture from the oven. Mix well and place into containers to freeze.

SECOND WAY

6 cups chopped strawberries

3 cups sugar

Place strawberries and sugar in a large glass bowl. When the sugar melts and mixes with the fruit, move it to a stovetop pan and boil about 7 minutes. Then, spread it out in a few Emile Henry–type baking dishes and leave them in a convection oven for several hours, until it thickens. Pull them out, place the jam in small containers and freeze it.

Mrs. Horner's Blackcurrant Jam

I have never made this, but I have eaten it and found it quite lovely.

3 cups blackcurrants

2 cups water

5 cups sugar

Boil and stir the blackcurrants and water for about 10 minutes. Add sugar and boil for 3 minutes. Cool and freeze, or follow the directions in a good canning book.

Tomato Jam

This is amazing with cheeses!

★ **You can always add more, but you can't remove ingredients. Taste and smell as you go with everything you cook.**

1 large can organic tomatoes, crushed

6 fresh tomatoes, roasted

Lots of garlic and onion

Brown sugar

Apple cider vinegar

Balsamic vinegar

Pinch of star anise

Fresh basil

Oregano

Thyme

Marjoram

Combine ingredients and cook until thickened and reduced.

Basil Macadamia Nut Oil Dressing

We first had this dressing in Maui and we loved it.

1 cup basil

2 to 3 cloves garlic, grated

Handful of toasted macadamia nuts

Rice vinegar

Macadamia oil, to taste

Romano cheese

Process all ingredients in a food processor. Serve over a green salad.

Lisa's Dressing

My daughter Lisa shared this with me. She is a really skilled cook.

★ This dressing is also wonderful with noodles and fresh veggies, topped with chopped nuts.

½ cup peanut butter

1 tbsp honey

1 cup boiling water

6 tbsp cider vinegar

2 tsp garlic, minced

1 tbsp sesame oil

1 tbsp soy sauce

1 tsp sherry

A small amount of hot sauce

Chopped peanuts

Mix all ingredients except the peanuts in food processor. Add in the peanuts, then use on your salad.

Don't Forget the Sauce

IT'S 4:30 P.M. ON a warm autumn afternoon and I have offered to bring my grandmother's mustard sauce to my friends' home for Thanksgiving dinner. Lou is serving ham, and I can't eat ham without this amazing mustard sauce.

The problem is I can't find the recipe. I panic because I sort of know what's in it but it would be nice to glance at the original recipe. But then I find it: the recipe is in my original book, *Red River Remembered*. I run up to my office, crawl under my desk and pull the book out of an old box.

In just a little while, the sauce is made and in a jar, ready for transport.

Mustard Sauce

Mustard sauce is a must if you are serving ham!

1 cup sugar

½ cup white vinegar

2 or 3 eggs

2 tbsp mustard powder

2 tbsp water

Pinch of salt

Combine all of the ingredients and cook on the stovetop. Stir constantly until thickened or microwave, watch and stir.

Highlevel Diner Ketchup

Many years ago, I asked one of the then owners of this diner for the ingredients in their famous ketchup. This is the list she gave me.

Onions

Garlic

Oregano

Brown sugar

White vinegar

Worcestershire sauce

Tomato paste

Pimento

Crushed tomatoes

Put all the ingredients in a pot and cook. This is truly wonderful with fries.

Quick Dills

I have made dill pickles in the past that have been so-so. This year I decided to just make a few jars of quick dills to keep in the fridge and enjoy in the early autumn. These are really good! They keep about one month in the fridge.

★ Always use pickling cucumbers for these, not regular cucumbers. And the vinegar must be 5% acidity—use pickling vinegar.

Pickling cucumbers, cut into quarters

2 heads of dill

2 cloves garlic

1 cup water

1 cup white vinegar

2 tsp dill seeds

Pack pickling cucumbers in clean, warm jars and top with dill and garlic. Make a brine of the remaining ingredients and pour the hot brine overtop of the pickles. Cool and refrigerate.

Yam Chips

TWO WAYS

I first had these yummy delights at my friend Marion's house. She served them with a salad and white fish. These are two of my versions.

FIRST WAY

8 yams, peeled and sliced like chips

Good olive oil, infused with garlic

A pinch of cumin

Paprika

Sea salt

DIP

Mayonnaise

1 clove garlic, minced

½ red pepper (from a jar)

Parmesan, grated

Toss all main ingredients together until completely coated. Bake on a cookie sheet in a hot oven until done. Keep an eye on them to prevent over-browning. Mix the dip ingredients in a food processor and serve on the side.

SECOND WAY

Prepare as with the first way, but for spices use paprika, thyme, rosemary and chives. Top with sea salt. For a dip, mix Miracle Whip, roasted garlic, pitted and ground kalamata olives, lemon juice and onion powder.

★ **Another great way to prepare yams is to peel and slice them, then cook to al dente. Let cool, and toss in orange juice, thyme and chopped hazelnuts. Finish by sautéing in butter.**

Basil Pesto

TWO WAYS

The first way is my own classic recipe. The second way adds a bit of a Hawaiian twist.

★ **If you want to make your pesto into a dressing, use rice wine vinegar and reduce the spinach and other solids to keep it more liquid.**

FIRST WAY

Lots of basil

Lots of spinach (to extend the basil and keep the pesto green)

Nuts (I like either walnuts or almonds), toasted

Olive oil, the best you can afford

Cheese (I generally use a combination of whatever I have on hand)

Lots of garlic

Put it all in the food processor and zap—it's done! Store in freezer bags in the freezer or, to better preserve the quality, use a vacuum packer.

SECOND WAY

Use the same ingredients and method as the first way, except use macadamia nuts and macadamia oil instead of olive oil and cheese.

Basil Bonanza

IT IS A HOT summer day in the Kootenays. We are in a small village called Fauquier. It is the home of Don's parents, and we have come to help harvest the fruit trees and chop wood for the chilly winter ahead.

I wander through the large garden, so robust and green. The plants look so much healthier than the ones back home in Alberta, where we recently battled an August frost. I leave the main garden and walk around the side of the house, where Mrs. Horner keeps her herbs. All of a sudden, I see it. Basil! Beautiful, bountiful basil. I can hardly believe my eyes. I reach out, pull a leaf and press it between my fingers to be sure. Yes, it is basil! Rows, easily a metre high, like I have never seen before. Clearly it is time to make pesto.

I run into the house and ask Mrs. Horner what she plans to do with all her basil. She says she isn't sure what to do with these strange, tall plants.

After a quick meeting with Don, we are off to the next town to buy the best ingredients we can find for pesto. We arrive back at the house, laden with our pesto-making ingredients. That summer we make many, many batches of pesto, for both the Horners and for our freezers!

Pastry

A simple, classic pastry recipe you can use for almost anything.

5 cups flour

1 lb lard

1 egg, beaten

Cold water

White vinegar

Beat an egg in a measuring cup, fill almost to 1 cup with cold water, then top up with about 2 tbsp of vinegar to total 1 cup. Add mixture to your food processor with flour and lard.

Mix briefly, form into balls and freeze.

Yogurt Cheese

This stuff is amazing. Even the dog loves it! You'll need to buy a yogurt cheese maker at your local kitchen shop. They usually cost about $20—a good investment.

1 large container of plain, low-fat yogurt

Put a large container of yogurt in the container of the yogurt cheese maker and wait. In about a day, you will have yogurt cheese! Eat it by itself, or use it as a replacement in recipes that call for cream cheese.

★ **The yogurts I like best are Liberté or Fraser Meadow; both are organic. The yogurt you choose must have active bacterial cultures to work properly.**

Labour Day Tomato Sauce

This is a basic tomato sauce I use for many things.

★ **You can add other things, too, as you come to the end of the simmering.**

About 20 soft tomatoes, chopped

2 heads garlic, chopped

1 large Walla Walla onion, chopped

One head fennel, chopped

A glug of red wine

1 capful of Pernod

1 jar of a good-quality tomato sauce (I like Stonewall Kitchen Roasted Garlic Basil)

Oregano

Salt and pepper

Simmer all ingredients together. It will be quite liquid when you start, but after several hours of simmering, it really cooks down. At that time, modify your seasonings to taste.

Labour Day at the Market

ONE SEPTEMBER LONG WEEKEND, we are in Vancouver, which means a trip to the Trout Lake market, one of my favourite farmers' markets. In our family, whenever possible, Saturdays begin with such a trip, followed by a lazy breakfast at one of our local bistros.

Trout Lake Farmers' Market is so Vancouver—almost everything is organic and they are proud of it. The market is rich with granola culture. People dress in semi-hippie attire and generally the love flows. A vendor I particularly like is covered in tattoos, with her flowing hair tied back in a knot and her reading glasses strung with rickrack, the stuff my grandmother trimmed her aprons with.

By the end of our trip, our cloth market bags are bulging with fresh organic produce—spinach, basil, lettuces in several varieties, Walla Walla onions, garlic, many varieties of tomatoes, corn, mushrooms (wild and domestic), small Pontiac potatoes, beans, broccoli, carrots in several colours, beets, Swiss chard, squash (both summer and winter), raspberries, strawberries, blueberries, blackberries, cherries and peaches.

At home, I make both raspberry and blackberry jam. Some of the fruit will be eaten fresh and some will find its way into crisps and free-form pies to be frozen and enjoyed later. About half the carrots and broccoli are mixed with organic beef and buffalo meat for Misha. The basil and spinach are made into pesto and frozen. The soft tomatoes find themselves in a sauce. The whole Labour Day weekend is filled with processing the treasures we have brought home from the market.

Master Mix

Everything is easy when you have this Master Mix on hand. This is one of my most valuable recipes, and on many occasions, it has bailed me out. I use it for pancakes, waffles, scones and so many other things. In our vacation home on Pender Island, I store Master Mix in the freezer, and it is also a handy thing to have on a camping or boating trip. Last summer Don and his brothers took a double batch on a boating trip.

6 cups flour

3 tbsp baking powder

1 tbsp salt

¾ tsp cream of tartar

⅓ cup sugar

1 cup butter

1 cup dry milk powder (I like buttermilk powder)

1 egg

Milk or water

Mix everything except the milk and egg in a food processor. At this point, you can store the mixture in the fridge or freezer until you are ready to use it.

When you are ready to bake, add the egg and enough milk or water to create the balance you need—this will change depending on whether you are making pancakes, scones, et cetera. A good starting point is 2 cups of dry to 1 cup of wet.

★ **Do not overmix!**

Presentation and Garnitures

Put flowers on the table, low and in different vessels. On the buffet table, you can vary the heights using blocks of wood to elevate and protect the table.

When serving seafood in a buffet, be mindful of food safety. Always use a "double dish." For example, prawns in a bowl should be placed in another bowl that's filled with ice. I have wrapped an ice pack and placed it on a tray, then placed a salmon mousse on top. Remember to keep the cold things cold and the hot things hot.

Keep your candles low.

Always garnish puréed soups with something like parsley, crème fraiche or flavoured oils. For a squash soup, maybe use some roasted apple and crisp sage.

Serve cherry tomatoes with a sprig of rosemary or parsley on the side.

When serving mustards and chutneys, use three matching ramekins; always go for an odd number. If you are at a loss as to what to put in the third bowl, toss in some olives. They go with just about anything!

Jelly and jams can be served in interesting pots or an old glass sugar bowl.

Always brown your butter when serving perch, sole or trout. Top with capers and a splash of white wine or vermouth.

Edible flowers and parsley—both curly and Italian—are always a wonderful garnish on just about anything.

Buy a few large, interestingly shaped serving platters. Go white if you can, as it shows the food off the best.

Serve salads in something unexpected. Once I served a light green salad in a pottery jar and used garlic scapes as a garnish.

Try serving your squash mash in a carved-out pumpkin.

At Christmastime, top casseroles with pomegranate seeds and chopped parsley or mint.

Large, flat wicker baskets are great for breads, muffins or buns; just line the basket with a tea towel or overlapping cloth napkins.

Use different types of cloths for your table. For years I used a bedspread. It was quite wonderful!

When plating cookies, sandwiches or filled buns on a plate, do not overcrowd. Line in orderly rows.

Cut the crust off open-faced sandwiches and vary the shapes.

For children's sandwiches—like grilled cheese—use a cookie cutter to create different shapes. Even a circle shape would be fun!

When serving pizza, top with something fresh like arugula, parsley, roasted garlic, green onions or fresh tomatoes prior to serving.

Prepare layered puddings in small juice glasses, then top with fruit, chocolate chips, spun sugar or mint leaves. Other desserts can be served in martini glasses.

Desserts, appies and soups can be served in small preserving jars for interest. They're also easy to transport this way: just use the box the jars came in and top them with their lids.

Be sure the ice cubes in the freezer are fresh.

Can This Be Love?

ON OUR FIRST DATE I am all dressed in black—jacket, sweater, culottes, tights and boots. And, of course, black leather gloves. He makes me laugh and laugh, which is fun.

He asks our mutual friend, "Does she always wear black?"

"Yes, mostly," our friend answers. My date is used to more colourful women.

Our friend is correct. We have met at a time in my life when I do mostly wear black. Upon reflection, I'm not sure if it is lack of funds, or an attempt to look sophisticated, or just plain sadness. At this time my dad is dying. I am single and alone and afraid because I've never found "me." Alone, because the people I'd loved and trusted most have died, leaving me with my two beautiful daughters, who are also attempting to find their way in the world.

After this first date, I don't see or hear from him again for a month.

But then, every month for a year, he surfaces and we have an adventure. A wonderful adventure filled with laughter and fun. Two people learning to be friends. One summer evening we are driving along a side street in the downtown area and a song comes on the radio that I love. He stops the car—double-parks—and we dance on the road, laughing so hard I can hardly remain upright.

Shortly after Dad dies, we go on a Sunday afternoon hike in the Edmonton River Valley. As the sun begins to drop, he gives me three choices—we can have dinner at a restaurant, he can cook dinner for me at his place or we can have a wiener roast and champagne in the river valley. I choose the wiener roast. (Even now, years later, give me a hot dog on a stick and a fire, and I'm a happy camper. Interesting how we associate food with our life events, both positive and negative.)

The warm summer days that follow include sailing on a nearby lake, picnics and breakfasts. One breakfast date ends in a trip to Costco (my first of many to come).

Autumn brings lunches of sushi and dinners with long visits. It is a time to get to know each other.

When the snow arrives, so does a pre-Christmas visit to see the holiday lights at the Legislative Building. There is laughter and merriment as we throw snowballs at each other and run through the fresh powdered snow. Closure for the date is at a warm bistro, where we have late-night candle-lit snacks of wine and pâté.

In the New Year things begin to change. I am his date for a very special dinner at a formal party at his club. We eat and dance until I can hardly walk and laugh the night away. I have no sense of rhythm but I love dancing. I just wing it and have fun! Driving home through the gently falling snow, I suggest we go tobogganing. And so we do, under the light of the full moon.

After a year of very casual dating we decide maybe we should become "an item." The adventures escalate and the friendship deepens. Love and respect comes to the table, and so, on a beautiful autumn day, I marry Don, the man who makes me laugh.

Noni's Place

We are here
The anticipated here
Past parade of flowers
Round the curve
To ocean view

All voices at once
Mix with welcoming woofs
So much news
So much to experience

Days happy with
Creative exchanging, garden exploring
Fountains splashing, feasting
Tired feet to fire crackling
Sharing our stories

Time to leave
We skim across the sea
Know the power of
Machine, Pacific and friendship

All too soon
Hellos become goodbyes

Marjorie Phillips
May 2012

Acknowledgements

I WISH TO THANK my good friend Marjorie Phillips for generously sharing two of her poems with us. These poems were written on Pender Island during one of our early writers' retreats.

Thank you to my daughter Lisa and her partner Dave, who have been with me every step of this journey, getting me hard copies and helping me work with my new Apple computer. And to Brian Dyck, the techie at Don's office. Many times poor Brian with his unwavering patience has listened to me as I threatened to throw my computer into the ocean.

Also, thank you to Joanne Dolan, who has typed and re-typed many copies of my manuscript for me. To my wonderful copy editor Melissa who went through every word with me, and to the publishing team at Page Two who helped bring this book to life. I am truly grateful to you all. Thanks so much!

Index

PHOTO BY DONALD G. HORNER

About the Author

NONI CAMPBELL-HORNER IS a writer who splits her time between Vancouver, BC, and Calgary, Alberta, with summers spent in the Gulf Islands. Her previous books include *Red River Remembered* and *Mikah Visits the Sea*.

Made in the USA
Columbia, SC
02 December 2022